Dreams & Visions

Divine Interventions in Human Experience

John P. Lathrop

Dreams & Visions: Divine Interventions in Human Experience

Copyright © 2012 John P. Lathrop. All rights reserved.
http://www.JohnPLathrop.org/

Cover by Joshua Paul King Photography.
http://www.JoshuaPaulKing.com/

Published by J. Timothy King.
http://www.JTimothyKing.com/

First trade paperback edition, September 2012.
ISBN 978-0-9816925-8-6

Printed in the United States of America.

10 9 8 7 6 5 4 3 2 1

Other books by John P. Lathrop

The Power and Practice of the Church
God, Discipleship, and Ministry

God, Discipleship, and Ministry: These are three of the major themes in the Bible. In this book, you will find 18 essays, articles, and sermons, which focus on the Lord's relationship with us and our relationships with one another.

This collection of sermons and essays reflects John Lathrop's manifest skill as a teacher of the Word: cerebral, full of substance, light on the clichés, thought-provoking and inspiring. He writes from a Pentecostal perspective, but pulls no punches when addressing myths common with Pentecostalism. He opens the scriptures to us as an experienced pastor, well-read, addressing significant and sometimes controversial issues within the church, including the gifts of tongues and prophesy, divine guidance, spiritual conceit, women in church leadership, collecting offerings, and Jesus as a model for the church's public ministry.

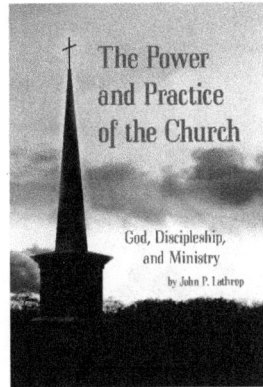

Answer the Prayer of Jesus
A Call for Biblical Unity

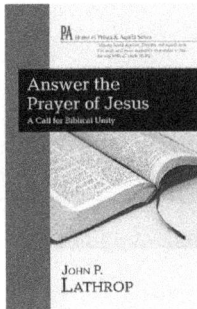

God has accomplished many great things through the church, but can the church be even more effective? Is there something the church can do to be both more pleasing to the Lord and more productive?

The church can be more effective in its mission if it seeks to answer the prayer of Jesus in John 17, his prayer for unity. This book examines both the challenges and possibilities of unity. Drawing from Scripture and his experiences of contemporary church life, John Lathrop gives specific examples of unity, and offers practical advice about how one can become part of the answer to the prayer of Jesus. This book will enable you to see a small portion of what God is doing in the world today and will encourage you to become part of it.

Apostles, Prophets, Evangelists, Pastors, and Teachers Then and Now

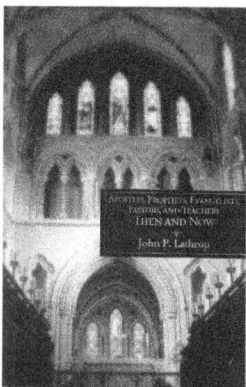

Paul tells us that Jesus gave apostles, prophets, evangelists, pastors, and teachers to the church... in the days of the New Testament. But does he still give all of them to the church today?

In this book you will find: • The ministries of apostles, prophets, evangelists, pastors, and teachers defined. • Names of people in the Bible who held these ministries. • Descriptions of each ministry from a biblical-historical perspective. • An examination of the contemporary expressions of the ministries of evangelists, pastors, and teachers. • Answers to objections about the presence of apostles and prophets in the church today. • A case for the continuance of the ministries of apostles and prophets in the modern church. • A description of the ministries of apostles and prophets in the contemporary church.

Table of Contents

Part Three: Dreams & Visions in Modern Times

This book is dedicated to rekindling expectations for divinely inspired dreams and visions among people in the West.

Acknowledgements

I am blessed to have a circle of friends who have helped and supported me in the writing of this book. I would like to acknowledge their contributions. John Ames, who serves on the staff of The River Church in Waltham, Massachusetts, and my nephew, Jonathan Davis each read a portion of the manuscript, offered encouragement, and made suggestions for improvement. John King, my longtime friend, helped clarify my thinking about a part of the book that I found difficult to write. Dr. William Spencer also helped me in this way. My wife, Cynthia, and our friend Esmé Bieberly, served as my copy editors. I would also like to thank those who sent accounts of dreams and visions to me: Pastor Nancy Hudson, "Jake," "Marty," Dr. Constantine Murefu, Katie Pawlak, Pastor R. Loren Sandford, and Pastor Eugene Smith. Lastly I would like to acknowledge the help of my friends, Tim and Joshua King. Tim published the book, and his brother, Joshua, created the cover. Thanks to all of you! Your labors are appreciated.

Introduction

The Bible has been around for a very long time; it has stood the test of time and been widely distributed. The Bible is available in many different English translations and has been translated into numerous foreign languages as well. It is probably both the most loved and most hated book of all time. Its detractors claim that it is full of errors and contradictions, or that it is irrelevant. On the other hand, devout Christians believe that it is the Word of God. The doctrinal statements of many Christian denominations contain a statement to the effect that the Bible is the only reliable guide for faith and practice.

I believe that the Bible is the Word of God and that it was given to instruct and guide us. However, it must be admitted that it is not always an easy book to understand. There are a number of reasons for this. First, there is the matter of time. The Bible was written over the course of many centuries, in times that are very distant from our own.[1] This distance can create difficulties for us as we seek to understand what the biblical text is saying. Second, the biblical books of both testaments are set in cultures that are very different from our Western 21st-century culture. The cultures of the Bible sometimes have different thoughts than ours.[2] As a result, some of the cultural practices and understandings are foreign to us. Third, there are some things in the Bible that just *are* difficult to understand. For example, the apostle Peter said that some of the things the apostle Paul wrote about in his letters were difficult to understand (2 Pet. 3:15-16). If one inspired writer thinks that another inspired writer is difficult to understand, then you can be sure that it is true! Fourth, we should expect to find the Bible difficult to

---

[1] Gordon D. Fee and Douglas Stuart, *How to Read the Bible for All It's Worth* (Grand Rapids, MI: Zondervan Publishing House, 1993), 18-19.
[2] Ibid., 19.

understand at times, because the Bible comes from a God whose ways and thoughts are higher than ours (Isa. 55:9). We are finite beings trying to understand an infinite God; the creation trying to understand the Creator. Lastly, there are some things in the Bible that we do not understand because we have not had any personal experience with them. People in the Bible experienced them, but many of us have not, especially those of us in the West.

Writing about the empowering ministry of the Holy Spirit, Gordon Fee says that some people conclude that this dimension of the Holy Spirit's work does not exist today because they are exegeting their own experience, rather than the biblical text.[3] They use their own experience as a grid in interpreting the Bible, and their experience becomes the norm of what God does and does not do today.[4] This is certainly not the way that we are supposed to interpret the Bible, but the sad truth is that we can all be guilty of this from time to time. This is a potential problem, and all believers should be on their guard in an effort to keep from falling into this error. When Christians fall into this trap, they violate the evangelical tenet that the *Bible* is our only rule for faith and practice. In his book *Gift & Giver: The Holy Spirit for Today*, Craig Keener says that he has rarely witnessed miracles like those of Elijah, Elisha, or like the ones that we find in the gospels or the book of Acts; thus, based on his experience, he might conclude that such miracles do not happen today.[5] However, he goes on to say that it is his desire to see what the Scripture teaches and to attempt to bring his experience, and that of the church, more in line with the biblical norm.[6] This should be our desire as well.

Two areas of biblical experience that are often overlooked, or dismissed, today by a large portion of the church in the West are dreams and visions. We cannot deny that they were a part of biblical history; accounts of them

---

[3] Gordon D. Fee, *Gospel and Spirit: Issues in New Testament Hermeneutics* (Peabody, MA: Hendrickson Publishers, 1991), 119.
[4] Ibid.
[5] Craig S. Keener, *Gift & Giver: The Holy Spirit for Today* (Grand Rapids, MI: Baker Academic, 2001), 60-61.
[6] Ibid.

are found in both the Old and New Testaments. In other parts of the world, even today, dreams and visions are being experienced. For example, in Muslim lands many Muslims are coming to faith in Jesus because of dreams and visions. Heather Mercer, an American who lived for a while in Afghanistan, mentioned this in an interview that she did with Voice of the Martyrs.[7] Mercer was one of two Americans who were imprisoned in Afghanistan in 2001; her story is told in the book, *Prisoners of Hope: The Story of Our Captivity and Freedom in Afghanistan*. Kevin Greeson, who has ministered in large Muslim populations, also affirms that many Muslims are coming to faith in Christ because of dreams.[8] Philip Johnson reports that in churches of the global South, prophecy, faith-healing, exorcism, and dreams and visions are basic parts of the Christian faith.[9]

So why are dreams and visions considered a normal part of Christianity in the Majority World and less normal in the West? Aren't we are all reading the same Bible? Yes, we *are* all reading the same Bible. So why do we have such different perspectives and experiences? There are a number of possible explanations for why we do not typically accept dreams and visions as a normal part of Christianity in the West. First, there is the belief that since we have the Bible we do not need these other subjective, supernatural experiences.[10] Ex-cessationist, Jack Deere, used to hold this view with regard to the miraculous gifts of the Holy Spirit as well as dreams and visions.[11] It is, of course, true that the Lord does speak to his people through the scriptures, but I do not think that this line of reasoning negates the possibility of present-day dreams or visions. The Bible never places an expiration date on dreams or visions; there are no biblical texts that can be pointed to in order to support the idea that they have ceased.

---

[7]   See   "Heather   Mercer: On   Reaching   Muslims"; http://www.youtube.com/watch?v=ucvGi3q3alo; viewed December 3, 2011.
[8] Kevin Greeson, *The Camel: How Muslims Are Coming to Faith in Christ* (Arkadelphia, AR: WIGTake Resources, LLC, 2007), 11, 50.
[9] Philip Jenkins, *The Next Christendom: The Coming of Global Christianity* (New York, NY: Oxford University Press, 2002), 7-8.
[10] Jack Deere, *Surprised by the Power of the Spirit* (Grand Rapids: MI: Zondervan Publishing House, 1993), 14-15.
[11] Ibid.

Closely related to the first reason why dreams and visions may not be widely expected or accepted in the West is the fear of subjective experiences.[12] There is no doubt subjective experiences can be dangerous; it is possible for one, however sincere or well-meaning, to be deceived. The Bible speaks about false dreams and visions (Jer. 23:32; Ezek. 13:7), so this is a matter of legitimate concern. Not every subjective experience a person has is necessarily from God. One can be mistaken about the origin of a subjective experience. A person may think that his or her experience is from God, but it may not be; discernment is needed. Aids in discernment include the scriptures, the Holy Spirit's gift of distinguishing between spirits (1 Cor. 12:10), and the counsel of mature believers.

In addition, some believers may avoid these subjects altogether. They do this in reaction to other Christians who place a very heavy emphasis on dreams and visions. Those who avoid the topics of dreams and visions are trying to steer clear of what they perceive to be an extreme. In the process, they cut themselves off from two biblical ways in which the Lord may communicate with them.

The last reason that I suggest is one that I mentioned earlier, namely, that many believers in the western church have not experienced divinely inspired dreams and visions. This can be a major hurdle to accepting these acts of God. Hopefully a fresh look at the biblical texts will help renew a biblical expectation and experience of these revelatory phenomena.

In this book, we will examine the dreams and visions found in the New Testament. The *Dictionary of Biblical Imagery* indicates that both dreams and visions were recognized by ancient peoples but distinguishing between the two is sometimes difficult.[13] Dreams seem to be nighttime events, and visions typically take place during the day.[14] Categorizing night visions is more difficult.[15] Were they dreams or visions? As we proceed through this study, I will note texts where there is some question about whether a particular

---

[12] Robert Heidler, *Experiencing the Spirit* (Ventura, CA: Regal Books, 1998), 20.
[13] Leland Ryken, James C. Wilhoit, et al., *The Dictionary of Biblical Imagery* (Downers Grove, IL: InterVarsity Press, 1998), s.v. "Dreams, Visions," 217.
[14] Ibid.
[15] Ibid.

experience was a dream or a vision.

We will begin our study by examining the dreams of the New Testament. We will do this by taking them in the order in which they appear beginning in Matthew's gospel (which is also their historical order). After an examination of the biblical text of each dream, I will provide a brief "insights" section. In this section, I will highlight some of the things we can learn from each dream. I will be calling attention to what we can learn about how the Lord works in dreams.

After we complete our study of dreams, we will give our attention to the visions of the New Testament. We will do this in sections. First, we will look at the visions in the gospels, taking them in historical order (which in this case is not the same as the order in which we encounter them in the New Testament), and then we will look at the visions in the book of Acts, again taking them in historical order. Lastly, we will look at some miscellaneous references to visions which, for the most part, are found in other books in the New Testament. After we examine the biblical text of each vision, I will again have a brief "insights" section in which I will point out some of the things we can learn from each vision and how God works in them.

In the Bible, dreams and visions were given for very specific purposes. Though the purpose of each was different, there are at least four things that all New Testament dreams and visions seem to have in common: all were communications that came from God, all contained audible elements, all contained visual elements, and there is no biblical evidence that anyone who received a dream and vision sought these *specific* experiences. The details of each person's situation are not as clear to us as Gideon's. Scripture tells us that Gideon sought a very specific kind of guidance. His experience with the fleece, while it did not include a dream or vision, illustrates the point I am trying to make. We know he was looking for a specific kind of answer from the Lord (Jud. 6:36-40). He set the terms of how the Lord should answer him, but we cannot say that about those who received dreams and visions in the New Testament. If the people of the New Testament were seeking dreams and visions, we are not told about it. Dreams and visions are but two of a number of different ways in which the Lord can communicate with his people. For reasons known only to him, the Lord chose to communicate with the people in our texts by these two means.

After we have considered the New Testament texts regarding visions, I will cite examples of dreams and visions that have taken place in recent times. In addition to looking at these accounts, we will note the things that took place as the recipients acted on the revelations they received. The examples in this section come from information supplied to me by people in my network of friends as well as the writings of a few more well-known individuals. I will close the book by offering suggestions of how we, in the West, may reclaim dreams and visions as legitimate communications from God.

As we embark upon this journey, I hope that you will keep your heart open to the fact that dreams and visions are two very real ways in which God can communicate with his people. I want to stress that I am not suggesting that believers should specifically seek these things, but rather that we should be open to them (there is a difference). What we expect, in some measure, determines what we will receive. Dreams and visions are biblical, and God says that they will take place in the last days (Acts 2:16-17). According to the writer of the letter to the Hebrews, the last days began in Christ.[16] Hebrews 1:2 connects Christ with the last days. The last days will continue until the last day (John 6:39); we are thus living in the last days. Therefore, let us remain open to the possibility that we may experience dreams and visions in our lifetime.

---

[16] Craig S. Keener, *The IVP Bible Background Commentary: New Testament* (Downers Grove, IL: InterVarsity Press, 1993), 651.

Part One

Dreams in the New Testament

A Man's Dilemma

…an angel of the Lord appeared to him in a dream… (Matthew 1:20)

We do not have to go very far into the New Testament to find a reference to a God-given dream. There is an account of one in the first chapter of Matthew's gospel. The person who had this dream was a Jewish man by the name of Joseph; he was pledged to be married to a young woman named Mary (Matt. 1:18). In what should have been a very happy time in his life, Joseph found himself in a very difficult situation, a situation that was both socially embarrassing and potentially volatile. Mary, the woman he was planning to take as his wife, was pregnant before they were properly married according to Jewish custom, and before he had been intimate with her (Matt. 1:25). This would be a concern to any man who was about to be married, and Joseph was no exception. This pregnancy was definitely unplanned, and I dare say unwanted (at least by Joseph). The timing was all wrong, and the situation was troubling to say the least. The circumstances would have naturally raised the question, "Who is the father?" Joseph knew that he was not, but some of his family and friends might not be so sure. And worse yet, if Joseph was not the father, who was? Since Joseph had not had sexual relations with her, who had? Sexual intimacy with a man is the only possible way to explain Mary's pregnancy, right?

The Bible does not clearly tell us if Mary relayed to Joseph the events of Luke 1:26-38. If she had told him about the visit of the angel Gabriel and what he had said to her, Joseph did not believe it. Think about it, why would he? It sounds unbelievable. The story goes against nature, and there were no virgin births in earlier biblical history. There had been miraculous births before. Women who were beyond the age of childbearing or barren had children; Sarah and Hannah are examples of these women (Gen. 17:17; 21:1-7; 1 Sam. 1:5, 20). But there had never been anything like this—a child born without the involvement of a human father.

Matthew tells us that Joseph was a righteous person (Matt. 1:19). I am sure Joseph thought Mary was too. This situation shook him; in fact, it was so traumatic he was planning "to divorce her quietly" (Matt. 1:19). Doing this would in essence clear his name; if he went through with the marriage, it would be assumed that he was the father of the child. Divorcing Mary would send the message that he was not the father of the child and that Mary had been unfaithful to him.[17] Keeping the divorce private would protect Mary from public disgrace (Matt. 1:19). In spite of his own pain and confusion, Joseph was not interested in making Mary's life more difficult. He was a man caught in a dilemma, one he did not create, but that he had to deal with. I am sure he was both mentally and emotionally affected by the news of Mary's pregnancy. For Joseph, neither keeping Mary nor putting her away were pleasant alternatives. He must have wrestled considerably with the decision of what he should do.

How would Joseph respond? How *should* he respond? This was a major decision he had to make, and it would affect his life, Mary's life, and the life of the yet unborn baby. His consideration of divorce was certainly legal under the circumstances, and it seemed to be the natural and logical thing to do.[18] No one would have blamed him if he did divorce Mary, because she had apparently been with another man. But something took place, something so powerful that Joseph put the idea of divorce aside and took Mary home as his wife (Matt. 1:24) in spite of the messiness of the situation.

There was a divine intervention; it came in the form of a dream. An unnamed angel of the Lord came to Joseph while he was asleep and delivered an important message to him. The text says that the angel "appeared" to Joseph (Matt. 1:20). This indicates that there was a visual element in the dream; in addition to *hearing* the angel, Joseph actually *saw* the angel. Two of Joseph's senses were involved in this encounter: hearing and seeing. Though he was asleep and was not conscious of the physical

---

[17] Craig S. Keener, *A Commentary on the Gospel of Matthew* (Grand Rapids, MI: Wm. B. Eerdmans Publishing Company, 1999), 91.
[18] Ibid.

world around him, he was conscious of what was happening in the dream. We are given a pretty detailed account of his dream in our text. Let's take a look at the message the angel delivered to Joseph.

The angel made it very clear the message he was delivering was for Joseph. He called Joseph by name and identified his family line; he was a son of David (Matt. 1:20). The angel also identified Mary by name. Then he went on to speak specifically to the concern Joseph had been dealing with during his waking hours: Mary's pregnancy and how he should deal with it. The angel told Joseph the real story behind Mary's pregnancy. What he told Joseph was both incredible and true. The child that Mary was carrying was not the result of unfaithfulness; she had not been with another man; rather, "...what is conceived in her is from the Holy Spirit" (Matt. 1:20). This information was either a great revelation to Joseph, something that he had not heard before, or a tremendous confirmation of truth, if Mary had told him the story of Gabriel's visit to her (Luke 2:26-38). Either way it was an amazing story, especially since there was no biblical precedent for it, although it was foretold in Isaiah. 7:14. The angel then gave Joseph some additional information; he told him the child Mary would have would be a boy and that he was to be named Jesus. This was the same information Mary received when Gabriel visited her (Luke 1:31). Joseph's believed the angel's message and "took Mary home as his wife" (Matt. 1:24).

Insights

We can glean a number of important truths about dreams from this passage. First, we see that the Lord can communicate with people through dreams. I am not suggesting that all dreams are of divine origin, but some are; our text is a case in point. The Lord can send a message to people while they are asleep; he can reach them during a time when they are not actively seeking him. We do not need to be in a time of prayer for God to minister to us; God does not need an invitation in order to communicate with anyone. The Lord chose to speak to Joseph, not during an active time of prayer, but during a time of sleep.

Second, we see that the Lord does not have to be in a dream in order for the dream to be of divine origin. In our text, it was not the Lord who went to Joseph, but an angel, certainly one sent by him.

Third, our text shows us that some dreams can be very straightforward; that is, there is no symbolism in them that requires interpretation. A brief look at the dreams of Joseph, the son of Jacob, in the Old Testament (Gen. 37) shows that this is not always the case. The message the Lord sought to communicate in Genesis 37 required interpretation, and the dreams were not to be taken literally. In Matthew 1, the message of the dream was plain and simple. Joseph knew the message was for him and what he should do in his situation. The Lord apparently wanted to make sure Joseph could not, in any way, misunderstand what was said.

Fourth, our text demonstrates that God can speak to us about decisions that affect us as individuals, and other people as well. Joseph's decision affected his life as well as the lives of Mary and Jesus. There was a lot at stake here. This was a significant moment in salvation history.

Fifth, Joseph's experience shows us that the Lord can give very specific guidance through dreams. There was nothing vague in Joseph's dream. This should give us great hope; the Lord can do the same for us. If we are given divine direction through a dream, we need to do what Joseph did; he accepted the counsel and acted on it.

The insights that I listed above should not be seen merely as historical facts; they should be seen as principles of how God works in dreams. Not every divinely-inspired dream is going to have all of the characteristics that we find in Joseph's dream, but the insights we glean from this text are part of the truth God has revealed about how he works through dreams.

I need to add a word of caution here. In his book, *Prophetic Etiquette*, Michael Sullivant says that people should not expect that the gift of prophecy will operate for them "in every situation of life" or that it is the normal way for God to lead us through the decisions of life.[19] The same could be said about dreams. We should not live, or expect to live, our lives mainly on supernatural revelations such as dreams. Though the Lord may

---

[19] Michael Sullivant, *Prophetic Etiquette* (Lake Mary, FL: Charisma House, 2000), 100-101.

sometimes give them, and maybe more so during specific seasons of our lives, they should not be looked for on a daily basis. Our survey of New Testament dreams will show that dreams were usually given during times of special need. We have the Bible for our daily guidance and need to avail ourselves of its counsel.

Travelers' Redirection

And having been warned in a dream... (Matthew 2:12)

The next dream we come to is found in Matthew 2. The New Testament is off to quite a start with regard to dreams; within the space of 18 verses we have already encountered two divinely-inspired dreams. The recipients of this dream were the Magi. We cannot say for sure how many people were in this group because the Bible does not tell us. The Magi is an interesting group because they were not devout followers of the God of Israel; they were pagan astrologers.[20] They are not exactly the kind of people we would expect to visit the Jewish Messiah, but that is what they did.[21]

As Matthew 2 opens, we learn that Jesus had already been born. After his birth, Magi from the East arrived in Jerusalem asking where the one born king of the Jews could be found. Matthew 2:2 shows us that the Magi knew some important things. First, they knew that Jesus had been born. Second, although they did not call him by the name Jesus, they knew he was the king of the Jews. This was a truth Jesus would later affirm (Matt. 27:11). A sign that read "The King of the Jews" was also placed over his head on the cross on the day of his crucifixion (Mark 15:26). This sign stated the charge that was against him. The Magi were the first people in the New Testament to call Jesus the king of the Jews.

So how did they get this information? The Lord, through an angel, had earlier announced Jesus' birth to some shepherds in the fields shortly after Jesus had been born (Luke 2:8-20). During this encounter the shepherds were told some very significant things about Jesus; they were told that he is the Savior and that he is Christ the Lord (Luke 2:11). But the angel never told the shepherds that Jesus was the king of the Jews.

---

[20] Keener, *Background*, 48-49.
[21] Ibid., 48.

One early hint at Jesus' kingship is found in Luke 1. When the angel Gabriel visited Mary, he told her the child she would bear would be given the throne of his father David, reign over the house of Jacob forever, and that his kingdom would never end (Luke 1:32-33). The message is clear; the words "throne," "reign," and "kingdom" are all words associated with a ruler, in this case a king. Commenting on Luke 1:32, Darrell Bock says, "A king is about to be born."[22] In commenting on Luke 1:33, Bock says "… Jesus comes as King of the Jews."[23] This is true. However, the Magi were not present when this information was given to Mary, and it is doubtful that this news was made public.

It seems that in some way, unknown to us, the Lord let these men know that Jesus was a king. The Magi knew the right country to go to, but they did not know the right city. Craig Keener says that the Magi went to Jerusalem because that was where they would expect to find any Judean king.[24] If they had known and understood the scriptures, they might have gone to the right city, for Micah 5:2 indicates that a prominent ruler would be born in Bethlehem. So the Magi journeyed to Jerusalem and upon arrival declared why they had come: to worship the new king. As surprising as it may seem, our text shows us that these pagan astrologers had some true spiritual sensitivity.

The Magi's question regarding the whereabouts of the one born king of the Jews elicited quite a response. Matthew tells us that Herod and the whole city of Jerusalem was disturbed (Matt. 2:3). Herod was disturbed for a number of reasons. First, the skills of astrologers were respected in the Greco-Roman world.[25] Second, Herod was not from the proper family line to be king, and, as a result, many of the Jews hated him for being in that position.[26] Third, if someone was rightfully born to be king, then Herod's

[22] Darrell L. Bock, *Luke Volume 1: 1:1–9:50*, Baker Exegetical Commentary on the New Testament (Grand Rapids, MI: Baker, 1994), 114.
[23] Ibid., 116.
[24] Keener, *Background*, 49.
[25] Ibid., 48.
[26] John F. Walvoord and Roy B. Zuck, eds., *The Bible Knowledge Commentary: New Testament* (Wheaton, IL: Victor, 1983), 22.

kingship was in danger.[27] Fourth, on a practical level, you cannot have two kings in the same area.[28] Others in Jerusalem were also disturbed by the Magi's question; they may have been unsettled by the prospect of a lack of political stability.[29]

Herod wanted to know more about the one who was born king of the Jews, and he knew who to ask. He asked the chief priests and teachers of the law where the Christ was to be born. It is interesting to note that Herod associated the king of the Jews with the Christ (Matt. 2:2, 4). The religious leaders told Herod the Christ was to be born in Bethlehem. Their answer was based on a prophecy found in one of the Minor Prophets. In Micah 5:2, the Lord revealed that a ruler who would shepherd Israel would be born in Bethlehem. This information must have added some additional concern to Herod's already troubled mind because Bethlehem was only about five miles from Jerusalem.[30]

Armed with this information, Herod sent the Magi to Bethlehem to look for the child. He asked them to come back and tell him where the child was so he too could go and worship the one born king of the Jews. Herod led the Magi to believe that he had the same desires they did. The Magi went on their way, and the star that they had previously seen, which had been leading them, was once again visible. The star led them to the exact location where Jesus was. The prophecy and the star were accurate. The Magi went in and fulfilled their stated purpose for making the journey: they worshipped Jesus.

I suspect the Magi probably would have gone back and told Herod the child's whereabouts. After all, Herod was the king, and he also wanted to worship the child (or so they had been told). In addition, he had supplied them with information that helped get them headed back in the right direction.

However, they did not return to Herod; there was a change of plans. This change was not due to adverse weather conditions, a report of robbers

---

[27] Ibid.
[28] Keener, *Matthew*, 101.
[29] Ibid., 102.
[30] Walvoord and Zuck, 22.

on the road, or an arbitrary decision on the part of the Magi themselves: it was the result of a divine intervention. Once again, the Lord used a dream to make his will known. We are not given the details of the dream, and there is no account of it in the text. Neither are we told how many of the Magi had the dream; perhaps only one had the dream, and it was shared with the others. It is also possible that all of them had the same dream on the same night, but we cannot be sure. The only thing we do know for sure is that the dream contained a warning not to go back to Herod. Whatever the contents of the dream were, they were sufficient to impress the Magi to take an alternative route back home. Herod had sought to outwit the Magi; instead, they outwitted him (Matt. 2:16). They were able to do this because the Lord communicated with them through a dream. Though the biblical text does not say that the Magi's dream was from the Lord, the circumstances confirm that the dream was of divine origin.

Insights

The Magi's dream supplies us with some new insights about how the Lord works through dreams. First, we see that God can speak to individuals whom we might not consider to be genuine people of God. The Magi, while they journeyed to see the new king (Matt. 2:1), and worshipped him (Matt. 2:11), were very likely Gentiles.[31] They were thus, at that time, not a part of the officially recognized community of faith; they were technically not a part of the people of God. This dream, when placed alongside Joseph's dream that we looked at in the last chapter, shows us that God can speak to both Jews and Gentiles in dreams. He can speak to people who are part of the community of faith and those who are not. A person's spiritual history or ethnicity does not disqualify them from hearing from God. This text is one of a number of passages that shows God's interest in reaching out to the Gentiles.[32]

Second, this text show us that God can guide a group of people, who are probably not related to each other, by a dream (whether one of the Magi

---

[31] Walvoord and Zuck, 20.
[32] Keener, *Matthew*, 98.

had the warning dream or they all had the same dream). Though a dream is a private experience, the Lord can use it for his purposes to guide the public life of a group of people, as we see in this case.

Third, this passage shows us that divinely-inspired dreams can warn people of dangers that they are not aware of. I am sure Herod put his best foot forward and made every effort to conceal his true intent when he spoke to the Magi about finding the child, Jesus. I doubt that the Magi were able to detect Herod's evil intent at the time. But God, who knows the hearts of all people, knew what was in Herod's heart, and he warned the Magi not to go back to Herod. This is an important function of dreams because we cannot see everything with the naked eye. Our senses are limited; we cannot always discern peoples' real motives. In dreams, God can reveal information that is hidden from us.

We have just studied some very important events; they concerned the king of the Jews, the Messiah, Jesus. The Lord protected his Son from the plots and schemes of a cruel man, preserving Jesus so that he would not be killed before he completed his saving mission. The dream the Magi received was critically important.

Nighttime Emergency

...an angel of the Lord appeared to Joseph in a dream... (Matthew 2:13)

In this text, Joseph once again receives a dream from the Lord. As far as we know, this is the second divinely inspired dream that he has had, and he has had them in a relatively short period of time. He received his first dream while Mary was still pregnant. This second dream was received after the birth of Jesus. The exact amount of time that elapsed between Joseph's first and second dream is uncertain. It is safe to say he received the two dreams in the space of less than three years. This estimate is based on the length of Mary's pregnancy and Herod's directive to kill all of the boys in Bethlehem and vicinity who were two years old or younger (Matt. 2:16).[33] Joseph had his second divinely orchestrated dream shortly after the Magi had the dream that warned them not to go back to Herod. We know this because Matthew 2:13 says, "When they had gone, an angel of the Lord appeared to Joseph in a dream..." In context, the word "they" refers to the Magi. There was quite a bit of dream activity at this time as the Lord guided the biblical characters.

In Joseph's first dream, he was told not to fear going through with a specific course of action; namely, he was told not to fear taking Mary home as his wife. That dream helped him to make a very difficult decision. In this second dream, he was told to take action on something that was not yet in motion but was going to take place: the killing of the young boys in the area of Bethlehem.

Let us look at little more closely at Joseph's second dream. The directive Joseph received in this dream called for him to make a physical move; he was to take Mary and Jesus and go to a different location. In his first dream, an unnamed angel of the Lord appeared to Joseph and spoke to him; the same holds true in his second dream. In Matthew 2:13, the angel told him to

---

[33] Walvoord and Zuck, 23.

"Get up." These words, coupled with the fact that Joseph was having a dream, seems to indicate that Joseph was lying down and asleep. The message he received was basically, "stop resting and get up; you need to take action now; this cannot wait!" There was a great sense of urgency in the message. Joseph was instructed to take the child, Jesus, and his mother, Mary, and escape to Egypt. We cannot say for sure because the biblical text does not address this issue, but if the Magi told Joseph and Mary that Herod wanted to know Jesus' location because he wanted to come and worship him, it evidently was not a source of immediate concern to them. They apparently went to sleep for the night. The message the angel brought to Joseph indicated that Herod was a person they needed to be concerned with. Leave the country; flee to Egypt!

Joseph was also told why they were to flee; Herod was going to search for the child in order to kill him. The proof of this statement is found in Matthew 2:16-18. Herod's concern about the one born king of the Jews was so great that he was willing to kill other innocent children in his efforts to eliminate Jesus. In this passage, we get a glimpse of the Lord's foreknowledge and omniscience. The Lord knew what was going to happen; he knew what Herod would do once he recognized that the Magi were not coming back with the information he wanted. The dream is not the only thing that shows us the foreknowledge and omniscience of God. The fact that references to the events of Matthew 2 were written about in the Old Testament (Hos. 11:1; Jer. 31:15) also testify to the Lord's awareness of the events that were going to transpire. Matthew 2:14 fulfilled Hosea 11:1, and Herod's orders in Matthew 2:16 led to the fulfillment of Jeremiah 31:15.

Joseph took his dream very seriously; he responded to it immediately. In Matthew 2:14, we are told that Joseph got up and took the child and his mother and headed for Egypt "during the night." He did not wait until morning. From a human point of view, waiting until morning might have seemed more advisable. There are a number of reasons for this. First, at night the family would be sleepy and tired, so they would not be the best travelers. Second, it was dark, and it would be very difficult for them to see as they journeyed. Third, it was dangerous traveling at night; they could be attacked or robbed. However, our text does not give us any indication that Joseph objected to the instructions he had been given. On the contrary, he wasted no time obeying the directive he received. Joseph was also told that he and his family were to stay in Egypt until he received further instructions, which he did (see Matt. 2:19-20).

The Bible does not give us a lot of information about Joseph, but one thing we can say with certainty is that the biblical record shows he was a man of great spiritual sensitivity. He not only received guidance from the Lord, he acted on it. At times we may be tempted to stop short at the point of receiving guidance. The Lord tells us what to do, but we do not do it because it seems difficult or inconvenient. It is a general principle that divine revelation calls for a response. Whether one receives a revelation from the Bible, a prophetic word, or a dream or a vision, God does not communicate with us so that we can ignore him. Joseph's response to the dream was immediate, and we can certainly understand why. First, he had a supernatural encounter in the dream, and second, it was a life and death situation: the preservation of Jesus' life was at stake. Here again, the issue is protecting Jesus from Herod—preserving the Messiah from death before he accomplishes his atoning mission. Joseph's actions indicate that he definitely had respect for dreams. He accepted them as one of the ways in which the Lord guides his people.

Insights

Joseph's dream, like the Magi's, was a warning dream. God alerted Joseph of impending danger. The difference between the two dreams was that the Magi's warned them of what they should not do and Joseph's warned him about what was going to happen and told him what he should do. The dream we have studied in this chapter also offers us some additional insights into how the Lord works in dreams.

First, we see that through dreams the Lord is able to guard his overall program from being disrupted or destroyed by the plans of people. Herod was after the Messiah, but he was not able to get to him. The long-promised one was going to live to adulthood and accomplish all that had been written about him. Because people responded to divinely-inspired dreams, Jesus was spared.

Second, we see that God can use dreams to sovereignly direct our path so that important details are fulfilled. The preservation and placement of the holy family was absolutely crucial to the accomplishment of the purposes of God. This included such details as being in the right place at the right time (Matt. 2:22-23; see also Gal. 4:4). The Lord can do this for us as well. The times and places of our lives are under his control (Acts 17:26).

Unfolding Revelation

...an angel of the Lord appeared in a dream to Joseph... (Matthew 2:19)
...Having been warned in a dream... (Matthew 2:22)

In this chapter, we will be looking at two more dreams that Joseph had. The first came to Joseph in Egypt, the land he had been instructed to bring Mary and Jesus to (Matt. 2:13). Once again, we find that an unnamed angel of the Lord appeared to him and delivered a message. Please also note that his encounter had both a visual and an audible component to it. Dreams seem to have been the Lord's preferred method of communicating with Joseph at critical times in the life of his family. This is *not* true for everyone; the Lord works differently with different people. Joseph, as we have seen, was very responsive to dreams. All of Joseph's dreams concerned Jesus, his birth and safety.

There are a number of similarities between the dream Joseph had in Egypt (Matt. 2:19-20) and the one we studied in the last chapter (Matt. 2:13). First, the messages in the dreams were similar in form; Joseph was again told to "Get up, take the child and his mother..." (Matt. 2:20; see also Matt. 2:13). Second, the instructions he received called for action; he was to geographically move his family again. Third, the dream alerted him to something that he evidently did not know. This is understandable. When Joseph, Mary, and Jesus were in Egypt, they were a considerable distance from Israel. Since there were no mass communication systems in those days, news traveled much more slowly than it does today. Fourth, the reason for the move was stated; the angel of the Lord told Joseph that the people who were trying to kill Jesus were now dead. This news would surely have given Joseph confidence to make the trip back to Israel.

There was a difference between the two dreams as well. The difference concerned location, the place Joseph was supposed to take the family to. In Matthew 2:13, he was told to take Mary and Jesus to Egypt. In Matthew

2:20, he was instructed to take them from Egypt back to the land they had come from; they were to return to Israel. Matthew 2:21 indicates that Joseph promptly obeyed.

This brings us now to the second dream we are considering in this chapter (Matt. 2:22). According to the biblical record, this is the fourth dream that Joseph had; it is the third one he received in Matthew 2. He had this dream when he was back in Israel. Once Joseph, Mary, and Jesus returned to Israel, Joseph began to be concerned about their presence in the country (even though he had previously had a dream that instructed him to bring the family back there). He was concerned because he heard that Herod's son, Archelaus, had taken his father's place and was reigning in Judea (Matt. 2:22). The fact that a member of the same family remained in power made him afraid to be in Judea. Joseph was concerned for the safety of Jesus. His concern regarding Archelaus was not unwarranted; Archelaus also possessed the negative qualities that his father had.[34] The Lord addressed Joseph's concerns through a divine intervention; he gave Joseph a dream. We are not given much information about this dream. We do not know if an angel of the Lord or the Lord himself appeared to him in the dream. We also do not know the specifics of the communication he received; the words of the message are not preserved for us. What we do know is that Joseph was warned in the dream, and as a result he did not go to Judea, but rather to Galilee. Joseph was directed away from a southern area to a northern area; it seems the Lord fine-tuned Joseph's guidance. The Lord first got the family back to the land of Israel, and then he gave Joseph some more specific guidance. This was the second time the Lord spoke to Joseph in a dream when he had a specific concern that pressed on his mind (see Matt. 1:20). This dream not only brought Jesus to a safe place, it also brought him to the city of Nazareth in Galilee in order that he might fulfill a Messianic prophecy which said that he would be called a Nazarene (Matt. 2:23).

---

[34] Keener, *Matthew*, 113.

Insights

There is a lesson we can learn from the first dream that we studied in this chapter (Matt. 2:19-20). In this dream the Lord told Joseph that those who were an immediate threat to Jesus' safety, namely King Herod and his associates, were no longer a threat: they were dead. This shows us the Lord can use a dream to tell us that a danger has passed, so a dream can be given in order to comfort us.

Taken together, the two dreams we have considered in this chapter demonstrate that the Lord can give continuing guidance to his people through dreams. We have already seen this in some measure in Joseph's first two dreams (Matt. 1:20-21; 2:13), but this truth is drawn out even further by his third and fourth dreams. In these two dreams we see that in matters of great importance Joseph was directed to "the next thing" by dreams. He was not given all of the information at once; it was revealed to him bit by bit. It almost seems as though it was given to him on a "need-to-know basis."

In these dreams, we see that the Lord can give both general and specific guidance through dreams. In Matthew 2:20 the Lord told Joseph to take Mary and Jesus to the land of Israel. This direction was general, it was to a country, and Joseph obeyed. Once Joseph had returned to Israel, he became concerned because he heard that Herod's son, Archelaus, was ruling in Judea. There is a very important lesson here; in this passage we see the importance of using our minds and common sense as well as being open to the Lord's supernatural guidance. The fact that the Lord gave Joseph further direction confirmed that Joseph's concern, which arose as he thought about the situation, was justified. After this, Joseph received further revelation in a dream, and based on that revelation he moved his family to Galilee. This shows us that the Lord can give us more specific revelation when necessary to guide us to a place of safety. It also shows that he can bring us to the place he wants us to be in order to fulfill his purposes for us (see Matt. 2:23). One of the principles that emerge here is that we need to obey the Lord step by step. We are to act on what he is telling us at the time. When we do that, if there is further direction that is needed, the Lord will supply it.

Another thing worth noting here is that there is no limit on the number of dreams a person can receive; nowhere in the Bible does God set a limit. However, having said that, let me add a word of caution. *While the Lord can guide his people repeatedly or continually by dreams, that does not mean that he is going to do it all of the time for all of his people.* There is no evidence in the New Testament that the Lord led all of the people in the early church in this way. He did not do it then, and I do not believe he does it now. There are a couple of reasons for this. First, the Lord deals with us as individuals, so our experiences are going to be different. Second, constant revelation of this nature could be spiritually dangerous; in addition to becoming overly dependent on them, a person could also become proud. The apostle Paul wrote about a thorn in the flesh that was given to him in to keep him from becoming conceited because of all the revelations he had received (2 Cor. 12:7). The Lord wants his people to be humble, so he will work with us in ways that will cultivate that quality in our lives. We need God's help so that we do not neglect supernatural experiences, like dreams, and so that we do not become overly infatuated with them.

A Wife's Plea

...Don't have anything to do with that innocent man, for I have suffered a
great deal today in a dream because of him. (Matthew 27:19)

The dream we are studying in this chapter is the last dream mentioned
in the gospels; indeed, it is the last *specific* dream mentioned in the
New Testament. That is, it is the last dream connected with a particular
individual, in this case, Pilate's wife. It is interesting to note the time when
this dream took place. Pilate's wife had this dream just before Jesus was sent
to the cross. This means the dream was received near the end of the earthly
ministry of Jesus. It is commonly believed that Jesus lived to be 30 or 33
years of age. The dreams we studied in the previous chapters all took place
either prior to Jesus' birth or within the first few years of his life. Thus, it can
be seen that there was a considerable time gap between the dreams of
Joseph and the Magi at the beginning of Matthew's gospel and the dream
we find here in Matthew 27. The gap was probably at least twenty-seven
years in length. Based on the information we have in Scripture, it seems that
dreams apparently did not play a significant role in the plans and purposes
of God in the years between the events found in Matthew 1 and 2 and
Matthew 27. This is not to say there were not more divinely inspired dreams
during this time period. There may have been more, but if there were, the
Bible does not tell us anything about them.

The dream we find in Matthew 27 is unique among the dreams we have
studied so far. The other dreams were given to men; they were given to
Joseph and the Magi. This dream, however, was given to a woman: Pilate's
wife. The Bible does not tell us her name. This is probably because it was an
incidental detail; Jesus and his circumstances were the main focus of the
passage. The brief mention of Pilate's wife in Matthew 27 tells us that she
had a disturbing dream, a dream about Jesus. It is interesting to note how
she described Jesus; she referred to him as "an innocent man" (Matt. 27:19).

The Jewish leaders were accusing him of wrong doing (Luke 23:2), but that was not the case. The dream troubled her so much that she sent a message to Pilate, her husband, to warn him not to have anything to do with Jesus. The delivery of her message was timely; Pilate received it just before he passed judgment on Jesus' case. Pilate was warned, but he did not heed the warning. The pressure of the Jewish crowd proved to be too much for him, so he submitted to their wishes and handed Jesus over to be crucified (Matt. 27:22-26).

The biblical text does not say the dream Pilate's wife had was from the Lord. No mention is made of the things that we would typically expect to find in the record of a divinely inspired dream. We do not find any references to the voice of the Lord or an angel of the Lord. We are also not given the specifics of the dream; we are not directly told what Pilate's wife saw or heard in her dream. I think it is safe to assume that her reference to Jesus being innocent was a part of what was revealed to her. We do not know if this was plainly stated or whether she had to interpret the dream in order to reach this conclusion. We also do not know if she was told to warn her husband, but that is what she did. We are told the effect that the dream had on her: she suffered. In view of both the message she sent to her husband and the timing of its delivery, there can be no doubt that the dream came from the Lord. It was a divine intervention at a very critical time.

Insights

One of the lessons we learn from this text is that dreams are not solely the prerogative of men. The Lord can, and does, speak to women through dreams. We also see here, as was the case with the Magi, that the Lord can speak through dreams to people who are not clearly identified as people of faith. While I cannot speak with certainty about the religious convictions of Pilate's wife, there is no indication in the text that she was a believer in the God of Israel.

The latter part of verse 19, "Don't have anything to do with that innocent man, for I have suffered a great deal today in a dream because of him," shows us that Pilate's wife believed that what had been revealed to her was not for her alone. She sent the message to her husband. The message certainly had relevance to Pilate and the circumstances he found himself in at the time. We can glean from this that there may be times when the Lord reveals something to one person in a dream that he or she is to share with another person. Why the Lord does not communicate directly with some people in a given situation but rather works though others I cannot say. However, communicating by means of other people is also a sign of his care and grace.

One last insight concerning this dream is that the Lord can get his word to people in positions of governmental authority. Whether they believe and act on it is of course another matter. This completes our study of the dreams mentioned in the gospels. We move on now to the last, and only other, reference to dreams in the New Testament.

More to Come

...your old men will dream dreams (Acts 2:17)

The words of the biblical text I just cited were spoken in the city of Jerusalem during the Jewish Feast of Pentecost. They were part of the apostle Peter's sermon in the Jewish capital on that day. The words were not original to him; they were taken from a passage in the Old Testament book of Joel (Joel 2:28-32a). This text in Joel spoke of a future day when the Lord would pour out his Holy Spirit in a very extensive way. Peter cited the prophet's words in order to explain the events that had taken place on that first-century day of Pentecost. Some of the people who were in Jerusalem at the time said that the early Christians had partaken of too much wine (Acts 2:13). They said this after observing the behavior of the disciples who had been filled with the Holy Spirit (Acts 2:4-13). We are not told specifically what caused some in the crowd to draw this conclusion, but their assessment of the situation was wrong. Peter sought to correct this error by addressing it at the beginning of his sermon. He told the crowd that what they were witnessing was not the result of earthly indulgence but of a divine encounter. The disciples' behavior was not the result of being filled with wine but of being filled with the Holy Spirit.

The prophet Joel foretold this, a time when God would pour out his Spirit. Peter announced that the time had arrived. In fact, this was not a single day event. Acts 2:17 said that the outpouring of the Spirit was going to take place in the last "days" (plural). As I mentioned in the introduction of this book, the last days is a period of time. It began in Christ.[35] This time period will culminate on the last day (John 6:39). Further evidence that the outpouring of the Spirit is not a onetime event can be found in the book of Acts. In it we find a number of other occasions on which the Spirit was poured out (Acts 8:17; 10:44-47; 19:6). Two of the signs of the outpouring

---

[35] Keener, *Background*, 651.

of the Holy Spirit Peter mentioned were dreams and visions (Acts 2:17).

Brad Jersak says that Acts 2 shows us the beginning of a "flood of *revelation*" which includes prophecy, visions, and dreams.[36] So Joel's prophecy, cited by Peter, is a promise of more dreams to come. They can be expected. What is interesting is that in the remainder of the New Testament we do not find hardly any texts dealing with dreams. The man from Macedonia who appeared to Paul in Acts 16 may have been either a dream or a vision.[37] The text clearly says that it was a vision, but the fact that it took place at night leaves the door open for it to be seen as either a dream or a vision.[38] The same could be said about Paul's vision in the night in Corinth (Acts 18:9); the terms "dream" and "vision" are frequently used interchangeably.[39] Apart from these two texts, we are hard pressed to find other passages where dreams are mentioned or alluded to. This is not to say others in the New Testament did not receive dreams; they may have, but if they did there are no references to them found in Scripture.

Based on our text, someone might say that only men can receive dreams and visions because the verse says, "…your young men will see visions, your old men will dream dreams" (Acts 2:17). There are two things that can be said with regard to this. First, we have already seen that even before the outpouring of the Holy Spirit, God gave a dream to a woman (and apparently to one who was not even a part of the community of faith). Second, dreams and visions are part of prophetic activity, and God has said that both men and women can prophesy (Acts 2:18).[40]

In the next part of this book we are going to look at the visions of the New Testament. As we consider them, you will see that they share some common characteristics with dreams.

---

[36] Brad Jersak, *Can You Hear Me?: Tuning in to the God Who Speaks* (Oxford, UK, Grand Rapids, MI: Monarch Books, 2006), 21.

[37] John Stott, *The Spirit, the Church, and the World: The Message of Acts* (Downers Grove, IL: InterVarsity Press, 1990), 260.

[38] Ibid.

[39] Ryken and Wilhoit, et al., s. v. "Dreams, Visions," 217.

[40] Keener, *Background*, 328.

Part Two

Visions in the New Testament

A Brief Word About Visions

As we begin our study of visions, I would like to call your attention to the fact that more visions are mentioned in the New Testament than dreams. It is worth noting as well that a good portion of these visions are found in the book of Acts, which records the experiences of members of the early church. Why the Lord chose to include more accounts of visions in the New Testament than dreams I cannot say. Evidently it was because they played a significant role in the implementation and accomplishment of his overall plans and purposes.

As we study the visions, you will notice that they all contain a visual element, and, in most, if not all cases, an audible element as well (one vision which may not have had an audible element was Paul's vision in Acts 9:12). So, for the most part, those who received visions had two of their senses involved in the encounter. To me, the main difference between dreams and visions appears to be that dreams take place at night, or when a person is sleeping, while visions take place when a person is awake.

It is also interesting to note that the majority of visions that are preserved for us in the New Testament were given to apostles, specifically Peter, James, John, and Paul. However, this does not mean that visions were the exclusive domain of apostles. We will see that there was a priest, some women, and a person in the book of Acts, who as far as we know was not an apostle, who also received visions. In addition, we will see that the Bible leaves the door open for other people to receive visions as well. Let us turn our attention now to the visions of the New Testament.

An Old Man's Surprise

...They realized he had seen a vision in the temple... (Luke 1:22)

The vision we are considering in this chapter is not the first one that is found in the New Testament (there is one in Matthew 17). However, it is the first one in the New Testament time line and is the only recorded vision that took place before the birth of Jesus. This vision was given in the Jewish capital city of Jerusalem, in the Temple. The recipient of this vision was an elderly Jewish man named Zechariah. Luke 1:6 tells us that he was a man of good moral character; he was upright in God's sight and observed all of the Lord's commandments and regulations. His wife, Elizabeth, also had these same qualities.

Zechariah and Elizabeth were a couple that exemplified a significant spirituality. They were not nominally religious; they were zealous for the Lord and sought to honor and follow him. Zechariah was a part of the clergy of his day; he was a priest, from the division of Abijah (Luke 1:5).

One of the duties of the priests was to burn incense in the Temple; it was burned in an area outside of the holy of holies.[41] The burning of incense was a common practice in Near Eastern temples; in Judaism, incense was burned before the morning sacrifice and after the evening sacrifice in the Temple.[42] The times of the sacrifices were also times of public prayer.[43] We can see this in Luke 1:10 which tells us that "...all the assembled worshipers were praying outside." One day Zechariah was chosen by lot to burn incense (Luke 1:9). Due to the fact that there were a large number of priests, a priest might have the honor of burning incense in the Temple once during the course of his life.[44] The mere fact that Zechariah was chosen to burn incense, in and of itself, made the day

---

[41] Ibid., 188.
[42] Ibid.
[43] Ibid.
[44] Ibid.

special.[45] However, that was only the beginning of some special things Zechariah experienced that day. After he went into the Temple to burn incense, he received a vision. The Bible specifically calls his experience a vision (Luke 1:22).

In the vision, an angel of the Lord appeared to Zechariah near the altar of incense (Luke 1:11). The name of the angel was Gabriel (Luke 1:19). Gabriel later appeared to Mary (Luke 1:26-27). Based on what we have already learned about dreams and what we see in this text, it is clear that angels can appear in both dreams and visions. I doubt that Zechariah expected to encounter an angel in the Temple that day. Why would he? It was certainly not a daily occurrence. In this passage we are told how he reacted to the angelic visitation: he was startled by the presence of the angel "and was gripped with fear" (Luke 1:12). I imagine this would have been his reaction whether he expected to see the angel or not.

The angel saw that Zechariah was shaken by the experience, and so he spoke some words of assurance to him; he told him not to be afraid (Luke 1:13). After this, the angel proceeded to deliver a message to him. In our study of dreams, we saw that people who had dreams both saw and heard something; that is, two of their senses were involved in the experience. We find the same to be true here; there were both visual and audible elements in the vision.

Gabriel told Zechariah that his prayer had been heard. We cannot say for certain if the prayer the angel referred to was one Zechariah prayed while in the Temple burning incense or whether it is a reference to prayers that Zechariah had previously prayed.[46] Interestingly enough, the angel's message to Zechariah did not *seem* to concern his priestly ministry but was rather of a more personal nature; it concerned his family. The angel's message addressed Elizabeth and Zechariah's desire to have a child. Gabriel told Zechariah that he and Elizabeth were going to have a son. Darrell Bock has pointed out that the announcement of Zechariah and Elizabeth's parenthood not only answered their prayer for a child but also answered

---

[45] Ibid.
[46] Bock, *Luke 1*, 82.

Israel's prayer for redemption; prayer for the nation took place at the evening sacrifice.[47] The promised child would reveal the Messiah to Israel (John 1:31). Bock says, "God was tackling two problems at once."[48] The angel then went on to give Zechariah some very detailed information about this child who was to be born.

Gabriel told Zechariah the child was going to be a male and that he was to be named John (Luke 1:13). He was also told that the child would bring joy and delight (Luke 1:14), and would be great in the eyes of the Lord (Luke 1:15). This statement must have been especially touching for Zechariah to hear because he was a priest and had given his life to obeying the Lord wholeheartedly. In addition, Gabriel also told Zechariah how John was to be raised; he was never to drink wine or other fermented drink (Luke 1:15). While the word "Nazirite" is not found in the text in Luke 1, what the angel may have been telling Zechariah was that the child was to be raised as a Nazirite.[49] There is a difference of opinion about this.[50] For the specifics of the Nazirite vow, see Numbers 6. Even before his birth John was chosen to be a specially consecrated one. Additional proof of this is found in Luke 1:15; there we are told that John was to be "filled with the Holy Spirit even from birth." At the time this message was delivered, not many people in biblical history had been being filled with the Holy Spirit; it was the experience of a small number of people (after Pentecost in Acts 2 this would change). So, the mention of the fact that John was to be filled with the Holy Spirit is significant. The angel further went on to say what this child would do; he would bring many people back to the Lord (Luke 1:16). This was great news! Zechariah and Elizabeth would have been happy just to have a child, but the angel told them their child would be one who served the Lord. It doesn't get any better than that for a devout Jewish couple! If the story had ended after the angel's announcement that Zechariah and Elizabeth were going to be parents, it would have ended on a high note, but the story did not end there.

---

[47] Ibid., 82-83.
[48] Ibid.
[49] Ibid., 84-85.
[50] Ibid., 85.

In verse 18 we find that Zechariah asked Gabriel how he could be sure he and Elizabeth were going to have a child. We can certainly understand why he raised this question; what he had been told seemed impossible! Zechariah himself explained his reason for asking. He said both he and his wife, Elizabeth, were old (not to mention the fact that she was barren—see Luke 1:7). Their life situations made it almost certain that they would never have a child. So Zechariah questioned what he had been told. Because of his unbelief, he lost his speech for a period of time; however, his unbelief did not cancel out the message he had been given. Zechariah and Elizabeth did have a son; John the Baptist was born in due time and lived up to all that had been spoken concerning him.

Insights

When we studied dreams, we saw they did not need to have the Lord personally in them in order to be of divine origin; the same holds true for visions. In Zechariah's vision, it was the angel, Gabriel, who appeared to him, but the vision was still from the Lord (Luke 1:19).

We also learn from our text that the Lord can intervene in our lives and communicate with us in a supernatural way while we are awake, and he can do this without any advance warning. In Zechariah's case, the Lord waited until he was alone to do this.

Another lesson we can learn is that the information in a vision may not be only for the individual receiving it; it could be for others as well. The message Zechariah was given was not just for him but for his wife, Elizabeth, as well. The Lord can reveal something to us that he means for us to share with another person because the message concerns them as well.

This vision also teaches us that the Lord can communicate with us plainly in visions without using symbolism. This is not true of all visions as we will see when we get to Acts 10.

In addition, Zechariah's vision shows us that the Lord can give us very detailed information regarding what he wants us to know. Zechariah's experience also shows us that visions do not have to be warnings but can be encouraging. The Lord can let a person know about something good that is going to happen.

And last, we see that visions can take place in a religious setting. Zechariah's vision took place in the Temple, *the* religious place for the Jews. The Lord broke into the regular prescribed order of service in the Temple. The Lord can do the same in the church today. As we are participating in the regular worship activities of the church, the Lord can intervene in a supernatural way. For example, in his testimony, Kamran Yaraei, an ex-Shiite Muslim, recounts how he saw Jesus in a church service in Atlanta, Georgia.[51]

---

[51] Kamran Yaraei, *Testimony*, DVD (Fort Mill, SC: Morningstar Ministries, 2005).

Mountaintop Experience

Don't tell anyone what you have seen… (Matthew 17:9)

The New International Version translation of the verse cited above obscures the fact that the events found in Matthew 17:1-5 were a vision. It is obvious that something supernatural took place in the passage, but the word "vision" is not found in the text. However, the same Greek word that the NIV translates as "what you have seen" is elsewhere translated as "vision."[52]

The vision found in this passage of Scripture is the first one we encounter when we thumb through the pages of the New Testament, but it is not the first with regard to time. The vision in Luke 1, that we looked at in the last chapter, is chronologically the first one. That vision took place before Jesus was born, but the vision in Matthew 17 took place when Jesus was an adult and was carrying on his earthly ministry. As we begin our consideration of the vision in Matthew 17, please note that it took place approximately 30 years after the vision we looked at in Luke 1.

Christians sometimes refer to times of special revelation or intimacy with the Lord as "mountaintop experiences." Being on a mountaintop places one geographically closer to heaven, the place where God dwells (Ps. 115:3). Thus, if a person is on a mountaintop, they are in one sense closer to God. That is one explanation for the use of mountaintop terminology. There is, however, another reason for calling times of special nearness with the Lord "mountaintop experiences." There were people in the Bible who had close encounters with the Lord when they were on mountains. Moses on Mount Sinai is one example. Matthew 17:1-5 is likely another passage that has contributed to the coining of the term "mountaintop experience." The events in this passage were truly a mountaintop experience, both literally (since it took place on a mountain) and spiritually, as the disciples had a

---

[52] McReynolds, 1519.

close encounter with the Lord.

The mount on which this vision took place is oftentimes called "The Mount of Transfiguration," because Jesus was transfigured there (Matt. 17:2). A number of sites have been suggested as the place where the Transfiguration took place; possible locations include Mount Hermon, Mount Tabor, and Mount Meiron.[53] The exact location has never been determined with certainty.[54]

What we can be sure about is who was there. Four people ascended the mountain: Jesus, Peter, James, and John (Matt. 17:1). Peter, James, and John were apostles (Mark 3:14-17). These three men were the "inner circle" of the apostles.[55] They are referred to as the "inner circle" because they shared a number of experiences with Jesus that the other apostles did not. For example, they were present when Jesus raised Jairus' daughter from the dead (Luke 8:51-56); they were also closer to Jesus than the other apostles were when Jesus prayed in the garden of Gethsemane (Mark 5:37; Matt. 26:37).[56] Here too they share a special experience with him. Matthew 17:1 tells us that Jesus led these men up the mountain; it was his idea to take them there.

Once they were on the mountain unusual things began to take place. First, Jesus was transfigured before them, and his face and clothing became very bright (Matt. 17:2). Then two other individuals, who had not climbed the mountain, appeared. These two men were both from ancient biblical history. In the Bible, it is not common to find people from the past appearing at a later time in human history. The two men who appeared on the Mount of Transfiguration were Moses and Elijah (Matt. 17:3). The Bible tells us that Moses died and was buried by God (Deut. 34:5-8) and that Elijah, the prophet, was taken from the earth alive into heaven in a chariot (2 Kgs. 2:11). Both of these men were significant and highly regarded in Israelite history. In addition to their histories, which are preserved in the Old

---

[53] Joel B. Green, Scott McKnight, and I. Howard Marshall, eds., *Dictionary of Jesus and the Gospels* (Downers Grove, IL: InterVarsity, 1992), s.v. "Transfiguration" by W. L. Wiefeld, 835.

[54] Ibid.

[55] Ibid., s.v. "Disciples" by M. J. Wilkins, 178.

[56] Ibid.

Testament, they are both mentioned a number of times in the New Testament. These two men appeared and spoke with Jesus (Matt. 17:3). Luke 9:30-31, part of a parallel account of the Transfiguration, tells us that they were talking about Jesus' departure which was going to take place in Jerusalem. An account of what they actually said is not preserved for us in Scripture. What an amazing encounter this must have been for Peter, James, and John! I am sure that it was a lot for them to take in. The parallel passage in Mark 9:6 tells us that the disciples were frightened. But there was still more to come.

Matthew 17:5 tells us a cloud enveloped the group and a voice came from the cloud which said, "This is my Son, whom I love; with him I am well pleased. Listen to him!" God the Father identified Jesus as his Son and testified of both his love for, and approval of, him. He also told the disciples to listen to Jesus. There is no higher source of authority than that. The disciples heard the audible voice of God! Talk about open heavens! The disciples "fell facedown to the ground" (Matt. 17:6); the reaction of the disciples was understandable because they were "terrified" (Matt 17:6). Jesus touched them, told them to get up off of the ground, and not to fear (Matt.17:7). Jesus and the disciples then descended the mountain. What a powerful experience! Many years later, under the guidance of the Holy Spirit, the apostle Peter wrote about it (2 Pet. 1:16-18).

Insights

There are a number of things we can learn from this vision. First, a vision is not always focused on our needs or concerns; it can be taken up with glorifying Jesus Christ. He can be the main focus of a vision. That is certainly the case in Matthew 17; Jesus is the center of attention. He shows forth his glory as both he and his clothing become exceedingly bright. Moses and Elijah appear and begin to converse with Jesus, and he is the subject of their conversation. The Father also bears witness to his Son and tells the disciples to listen to him. The vision is thoroughly Christocentric. We could all benefit from a fuller understanding of the person and greatness of Jesus.

Second, the disciples' experience shows us that a vision does not have to take place in an area specifically set apart for religious practice, such as the Temple (where Zechariah received his vision). It is possible for the Lord to give a person a vision while he or she is in a church building, but the Lord is not limited to working only within the confines of recognized religious structures. God may come to us wherever we are.

Third, from the experience of the disciples on the Mount of Transfiguration, we learn that the Lord can give the same vision to a number of persons at the same time. A vision does not have to be an individualistic encounter. The apostles' experience also shows us that more than one person can appear in a vision.

The last insight that I will offer regarding this vision concerns timing. If a person has a vision, it does not mean that he or she should immediately rush out and tell everyone about it (as tempting as that may be). Jesus told his disciples that they were not to speak about the vision they had seen until after he had been raised from the dead (Matt. 17:9). Sometimes we need to wait before sharing things the Lord has revealed to us.

Sunday Morning

…they had seen a vision of angels… (Luke 24:23)

So far in our study of visions we have seen one that took place before Jesus' birth, namely, Zechariah's vision of the angel Gabriel in the Temple (Luke 1:11, 19, 22), and one that took place during Jesus' earthly ministry, the one in which Jesus was transfigured before Peter, James, and John on the mountain (Matt. 17:9). The vision on the Mount of Transfiguration took place before Jesus' crucifixion. The vision we are studying in this chapter took place after Jesus' crucifixion and resurrection. The events referred to in Luke 24 are recorded in other gospel accounts as well (Matt. 28:1-10; Mark 16:1-7). However, it is only in Luke's account that the appearance of angels is referred to as a vision.

This vision took place at the tomb of Joseph of Arimathea (Matt. 27:57-60). Joseph was a rich man, a member of the Council, and a disciple of Jesus (Matt. 27:57; Mark 15:43). He gave his own tomb for Jesus to be buried in (Matt. 27:60). The vision took place early on resurrection morning (Matt. 28:1; Luke 24:1); this was a Sunday, the first day of the week (Luke 24:1). The large stone which had been over the face of the tomb (Matt. 27:60), was rolled away by an angel (Matt. 28:2), thus making the tomb accessible. Some early morning visitors went to the tomb to anoint the body of Jesus with spices (Mark 16:1). While they were at the tomb, they encountered angels (Luke 24:23).

The gospel writer Mark refers to the beings in the tomb as men (Mark 16:5). Luke also does this (Luke 24:4). However, in Luke 24:23 he calls them angels. This should not be seen as problematic. Hebrews 13:2 says that "some people have entertained angels without knowing it." This text implies that angels can appear in human form. The glowing clothes of the "men" in Luke 24:4 indicate that there was something supernatural about them. The

Greek word translated "angel" can be also be translated as "messenger."[57] The beings at the tomb were most definitely messengers; they gave information and instruction to those who had come to the tomb in the early morning hours. The visitors who received the vision were women; those who came to the tomb on that Sunday morning were Mary Magdalene, Joanna, Mary the mother of James, Salome, and some other unnamed women (Luke 24:10; Mark 16:1).

In Luke 24:23, the vision is mentioned, not by actual eye witnesses of the event, but by some other disciples of Jesus who had heard the report about it. These disciples shared the report with the man they were walking with on the road to Emmaus. This man was actually Jesus, but at the time they did not recognize him. Luke 24:16 says that "they were kept from recognizing him." The vision they relayed to him was one of a list of unsettling events that had taken place over the past few days. In fact, it was a very recent event, having taken place that very morning (Luke 24:22-23). The vision and the empty tomb were not things that the women had expected; on the contrary, they had come to anoint Jesus' dead body (Mark 16:1).

The opening verses of Luke 24 give us a more detailed account of the events of the vision; they supply us with information that was not given in Luke 24:23. One of the things we learn about the vision concerns the appearance of the messengers; their clothes shone forth like lightening (Luke 24:4).

We also learn how the women reacted to seeing the heavenly messengers: they were frightened (Luke 24:5). This has been a consistent feature of the visions we have studied so far—everyone who has had one has been afraid. There has been something so "otherworldly" about it that it evoked fear.

The more detailed account of the vision also tells us what the messengers said to the women. They asked the women why they were looking for the living among the dead (Luke 24:5); then they went on to clearly state what their question had merely implied: Jesus had risen from the dead (Luke 24:6). Their words explained the empty tomb and agreed

---

[57] McReynolds, 956.

with what Jesus had earlier said to his disciples; he had told them that he would be raised from the dead (Matt. 16:21; Mark 10:34). This vision came at a crucial time when the disciples of Jesus were sorrowful and confused. It was one of the things God used to help turn the tide of fear and hopelessness among his disciples. God knows how to rekindle faith and hope in his people.

Insights

This vision also supplies us with additional understanding into some of the ways that the Lord works through visions. First, the Lord gave this vision to women. All of the previous visions we have looked at were given to men. This passage shows us God is not a respecter of persons; specifically, he is not a respecter of gender. The Lord can, and has, given visions to women. He did it in biblical history, as this text demonstrates and, as we will see later in the book, he continues to do so in our day.

Second, this vision show us that the Lord gives visions to people who are not in recognized positions of spiritual leadership. Zechariah was part of the official priesthood of Israel when he received his vision. Peter, James, and John were apostles who were being trained to be leaders of the new Christian movement when they received theirs. At the time the women received their vision we have no evidence to support the idea that they were in spiritual leadership, or that they were being trained for it. In saying this, I am not in any way suggesting that women cannot be in spiritual leadership in the Christian church; I am merely commenting on the situation of the women who received the vision in Luke 24. There were women in leadership in the first-century church, and I believe that women can be in leadership in the church today.

Third, the passage in Luke 24 shows us that the Lord can give a vision to confirm a truth that has already been stated: Jesus had previously told his disciples he would be raised from the dead. The empty tomb and the message of the angels confirmed the truth of what Jesus had said. All visions do not confirm previously stated truths, but this one did.

Fourth, this vision also shows us there are some visions that are to be shared immediately. The apostles on the Mount of Transfiguration had been told not to talk about their vision until after Jesus had been raised from the dead (Matt. 17:9). Matthew's and Mark's accounts of the women's meeting with the messengers indicate that the women were to go and share what they had seen and heard immediately (Matt. 28:7; Mark 16:7).

This concludes our consideration of the visions mentioned in the gospels. In the next chapter we will begin looking at visions that are recorded in the book of Acts. We will see that there are more visions recorded in Acts than in the gospels. Most of those who received them were believers, and they received these revelations at crucial times. As we consider the visions in Acts, we will take them in chronological order with one exception. We will defer consideration of the reference to visions in Acts 2:17 until a later point in the study.

An Interrupted Journey

...I was not disobedient to the vision from heaven. (Acts 26:19)

The vision we are considering in this chapter is not the first one mentioned in the book of Acts; however, it is the first one historically. The vision Paul was talking about in the text cited above actually took place back in Acts 9 when Paul, then called Saul, was confronted by the Lord Jesus. In the Acts 9 passage, the encounter is not referred to as a vision; in this account it is. New Testament scholar, Ben Witherington III, places the events of Acts 9 in either 33 or 34 A.D.[58] In Acts 26, as Paul stood before King Agrippa, he recounted what happened to him years earlier while he was on his way to Damascus; Paul gave his testimony. Paul's telling of the story provides us with information that is not found in any of the other scriptural accounts of his encounter with Jesus. This vision forever changed Saul of Tarsus and the course of his life.

Saul, also known to us as the apostle Paul, is a man about whom we know quite a bit. The scriptures supply us with ample information about him. A large portion of the book of Acts records his travels and ministry. In addition, we have his own writings that make up a large part of our New Testament. Passages that provide a significant amount of personal information about the apostle include Acts 22, 2 Corinthians 11, and Philippians 3. From these passages we learn about Paul's Jewish heritage (Acts 22:3; 2 Cor. 11:22); more specifically, we are told he was from the tribe of Benjamin and that he had been circumcised (Phil. 3: 5).

Scripture also tells us something about his religious life prior to becoming a follower of Jesus Christ. We are told he was educated in the Law by Gamaliel (Acts 22:3) and that he was a Pharisee (Phil. 3:5). He was religiously committed; to use his own words, he was "zealous for God" (Acts

---

[58] Ben Witherington III, *The Acts of the Apostles: A Socio-Rhetorical Commentary* (Grand Rapids, MI: Wm Eerdmans Publishing Company, 1998), 81.

22:3). His zeal manifested itself not only in his study of the Law of his fathers (Acts 22:3), but also in his persecution of the church (Acts 8:3; 22:4; 26:9-11; Phil. 3:6; 1 Tim. 1:13). During the time he was persecuting the church, he thought he was doing the right thing (Acts 26:9). Later he would come to see, and admit, that his actions were due to ignorance and unbelief (1 Tim.1:13). Only a serious divine intervention could change and redirect this young zealot, and the Lord gave him just that.

In Acts 26:12-13, Paul says that when he was on his way to Damascus, to persecute the Christians there, something significant and supernatural happened. This event stopped him in his tracks; it took place during the day, about noontime (Acts 26:13). He saw a bright light, fell to the ground, and heard a voice speak to him (Acts 26:13-14). According to Paul's telling of the story in Acts 22, the men who were with him saw the light but did not understand the voice of the one who was speaking to him (Acts 22:9). Paul said that he understood the language that was being spoken; it was Aramaic (Acts 26:14). He also knew who was speaking to him, for in response to his question, "Who are you, Lord," the speaker identified himself as Jesus (Acts 26:15). I am confident that this encounter surprised the young Pharisee. He had actively been involved in persecuting the church (Acts 8:3); he had put many believers in prison and had helped hand some of them over to be put to death (Acts 26:10). His encounter with Jesus would change all of that. The words Jesus spoke to him must also have been shocking, for the Lord not only identified himself, but he also told this persecutor of the church why he had had appeared to him. He appeared to him to appoint him as a servant and a witness (Acts 26:16). Saul/Paul did not object to this commission. There is no information in any of the accounts of his meeting with Jesus (Acts 9, 22, 26) that indicates he resisted the Lord's call and commission. He accepted what he had been told; he was a changed man. The Lord called this very unlikely person to become a Christian and to serve the Lord.

The newly chosen apostle was given some significant information on the day the Lord appeared to him. He was told he was to witness to what he had seen of Jesus and to what the Lord would yet show him (Acts 26:16).

The commission he received is in harmony with what the Lord had said to his earlier disciples (Acts 1:8). This verse also shows us that he would have a growing knowledge of the Lord and his ways.

In Acts 26:17, Paul tells us about some of the assurances the Lord gave him about his new ministry. The Lord told him that he would rescue him from both Jews and Gentiles. This statement was important because the Christian message was strongly opposed by some at that time. We see evidence of this in Acts, as early as Acts 4. Paul had firsthand information about the hostility that was sometimes directed toward Christians because he had personally been involved in persecuting the church. As he embarked on his new ministry, he would surely be opposed, but the Lord would protect him.

The details of what he was to do in ministry were also spelled out. He was to turn people from darkness to light, from the power of Satan to God, so that people could be forgiven of their sins and find a place among those who are sanctified (Acts 26:18). He was given a very significant mission: his ministry was to be radical and transformational. This can be been by comparing the things that people are turned from to what they are turned to. His mission field was also quite extensive; he was to minister to both Jews and Gentiles (Acts 26:17).

Paul told King Agrippa he had not been disobedient to the vision he had received. In Acts 26:19, he lists some of the places he ministered in: Damascus, Jerusalem, and Judea. He spoke to both Jews and Gentiles telling them that they needed to "repent and turn to God" (Acts 26:20). The history preserved for us in the book of Acts tells us some of what Paul did after his encounter with Jesus.

Insights

The first truth we can learn from this passage is that the Lord can give a vision to a person who has rejected Jesus, to one who has apparently closed both heart and mind to him. When the Lord appeared to Saul of Tarsus, he did not believe in Jesus. On the contrary, Saul was doing everything that he could to oppose the name of Jesus Christ (Acts 26:9). God is not bound to give visions only to believers (although believers may be more open to them).

Second, Saul's experience shows us that the Lord can give a vision to one individual and keep some of the aspects of the vision from others who are with him at the time the revelation is given; this was the case on the Damascus road (Acts 22:9; 9:7).

Third, from this passage we learn that the Lord can appear in a vision even after he has ascended into heaven. In Matthew 17, Jesus appeared in a vision during his earthly ministry, prior to his ascension. When the Lord appeared to Saul, it was after he had ascended into heaven. This is important for us to recognize because we all live after the ascension. He can still appear to us today!

Fourth, this passage also shows us that the Lord can state the purpose of a vision at the time it is given. In Acts 26:16, the Lord told Saul, "I have appeared to you to appoint you as a servant and as a witness." There was no question about why the Lord showed up (the Lord always has a purpose).

And last, this text shows us that the Lord can call a person to ministry through a vision (Acts 26:16-18). The information that the new apostle was given was not exhaustive, but it was sufficient to set him on the path to his new ministry.

A Tale of Two Men

...The Lord called to him in a vision, "Ananias!" (Acts 9:10)

In a vision he has seen a man named Ananias... (Acts 9:12)

In this chapter, we will be studying two visions that took place in the city of Damascus. Each vision was given to a different person. The two individuals who received these revelations were both Jewish men; their names were Ananias and Saul/Paul. Though these men were in the same city, they were not in the same location when they received their respective visions; neither did the two men receive the same vision. Each revelation was unique and specific to the need of the individual who received it. We will consider the visions in the order in which they appear in the biblical text.

The first person in our text to receive a vision was Ananias. This is not the same man we read about in Acts 5; that man was dead by the time the events of Acts 9 took place (see Acts 5:5). We know a number of things about the Ananias who is mentioned in Acts 9; Acts 22:12 tells us he was a devout observer of the Law and that he was highly respected by all of the Jews in Damascus. We get this information from Paul himself when he shared his testimony with an angry crowd in the city of Jerusalem. The Bible does not tell us how Paul came by this information. It is possible that Paul knew about him before he met the Lord on the Damascus road. I believe Paul learned about him after the man had ministered to him. The information we find in Acts 22:12 tells us that Ananias was serious about God and his faith.

In addition to his regard for the Law, he was highly respected by the people and was sensitive to the voice of the Lord. Unlike the young boy, Samuel, whom the Lord had to call a number of times before he recognized it was the Lord's voice (1 Sam. 3), Ananias recognized the voice of the Lord at once, and his response was immediate: "Yes, Lord" (Acts 9:10). This response, coupled with the fact that he is called a disciple, indicates he was a believer in Jesus. When the Lord spoke to Ananias, his initial communication with him was very brief; the Lord merely called his name, "Ananias" (Acts 9:10). His response was also brief, "Yes, Lord" (Acts 9:10). After this initial exchange, the Lord gave him some very detailed instructions. The Lord told him where to go and who to ask for; he also supplied him with additional information about the person he was sent to minister to. Ananias was told where the man was from, what he was doing, one detail about the man's physical condition, and the content of the vision that the man was seeing. Saul was blind, but it was only a temporary condition. Proof of this is found in Acts 9:9, which tells us that he was blind for three days, and Acts 9:12, which tells us Ananias was sent to Saul to *restore* his sight (Acts 9:12). This servant of the Lord was being sent on a very important mission.

Many of us might think we would like to have the Lord speak to us as directly as he did to Ananias. The message he received came with great clarity. However, his response to the Lord's *word* was quicker than his response to the *work* the Lord asked him to do. Ananias was not thrilled with the assignment he had received; this is clear from his words in Acts 9:13-14. In these verses, he proceeds to "inform" the Lord that the person he is being sent to is not a safe person to go to if you are a believer. Saul persecuted the church in Jerusalem and had come to Damascus to do the same to the believers there. By informing the Lord of Saul's history and intent regarding the church, Ananias hoped that the Lord would cancel his assignment to visit Saul. No such luck! In verses 15-16 the Lord responded to his objections and told him that Saul was his chosen instrument. Based on that information, Ananias made the journey and ministered to the persecutor of the church. As a result, Saul was healed, baptized in water, and filled with the Holy Spirit (Acts 9:17-18). This was a very significant and profitable divine appointment which Ananias kept because of a vision.

The second person who received a vision in Damascus was Saul of Tarsus. The account of his vision is very brief, and it is described in one verse (Acts 9:12). In fact, we know about it only because the Lord told

Ananias about it; this is the only mention of this vision in Scripture. Paul never made reference to it when he recounted his testimony in Acts 22 and 26. When Saul received this vision, he was physically blind. In view of this fact, it seems clear that he saw it internally, in his mind's eye. In the vision, he saw a man named Ananias come to him and lay hands on him to restore his sight (Acts 9:12). I wonder how Ananias felt when he learned that the Lord had already revealed his name and appearance to Saul in a vision (Acts 9:12). The Lord did not ask Ananias' permission before he shared this information with Saul! Talk about being put on the spot!

Insights

We can learn a number of things from these two men's experiences. First, we learn from Ananias' vision that the Lord can give very particular details in visions; the details in this vision are more specific than the ones Saul received in his vision of Jesus (as described in Acts 22 and Acts 26). The Acts 26 account contains a significant amount of information, but it is largely general in nature. In Acts 9, the Lord gave very precise information to Ananias: he was told whose house to go to, the name of the street it was on, the name of the man he was to ask for, and the physical condition of this man. Ananias' obedience to the vision resulted in the physical healing and spiritual equipping of a man whose life and ministry greatly influenced the church and the world, not only in the first century, but also in subsequent centuries as well. We too need to be obedient to the visions God gives us, first out of respect for the Lord, and second because we do not know how the visions we receive factor into his overall plans and purposes. God may send one of us to minister to a person who will greatly impact the world for Christ.

The second point we can glean from this encounter is that it is possible for an individual to have a dialogue with the Lord in a vision; it does not always have to be a one-way conversation. The Lord spoke to Ananias, and he spoke back to the Lord; then the Lord spoke to him again. So a vision is a "live" encounter; although it is somewhat mystical, it is nonetheless real.

Saul's vision in Acts 9:12 shows us that the Lord can reveal to a person how his or her particular need is going to be met. Saul had a vision of Ananias coming in to lay hands on him so that he would be healed (Acts 9:12). The vision was prophetic; it foretold what was going to happen before it actually took place. So we have our third point: visions can be prophetic; this involves not only foretelling but also encouragement. I am sure this vision was a comfort to Saul, in view of the startling events that had taken place on the Damascus road when he encountered Jesus Christ and was blinded. The vision assured him that he would not remain blind. The Lord can provide similar assurances to his people today.

An interesting fourth dynamic we find at work in Acts 9 is the Lord working with both Ananias and Saul to accomplish his purposes. He gave Ananias a vision to direct him to go to Saul so that the new apostle would be healed and filled with the Holy Spirit (Acts 9:17), and he gave Saul a vision to let him know help was on the way. The Lord gave each man the assurance that he needed. When the Lord works with us, he may very well be working with someone else as well in order to bring about his will. He frequently brings his people together for his kingdom's purposes.

Time to Move

...I fell into a trance. (Acts 22:17)

The words we have just read were spoken by the apostle Paul; they tell of an experience that he had. You may have noticed that the text cited above does not contain the word "vision." Instead, we find the word "trance" is used. These two terms are translations of different Greek words.[59] That being said, I think that what Paul described in Acts 22:17-21 was a vision. I say this for a number of reasons. First, the experience Paul mentioned in this text was a divine encounter in which he both saw and heard the Lord. Second, as we will see later when we get to Peter's experience in Acts 10, a "trance" was involved when he received a vision (Acts 10:10, 17). Third, in his commentary on Acts, John Stott referred to Paul's experience in this passage as a vision.[60]

In Acts 22, Paul shared a vision which he had received years earlier. The vision took place in the Temple after he had become a believer in Jesus. Paul shared this story with an angry crowd in the city of Jerusalem. The people were angry with him because they thought he had taken Trophimus, a Greek (a non-Jew), into the Temple and defiled it (Acts 21:28-29).

Paul had a number of supernatural experiences as a new believer in Jesus. The Lord apparently wanted to make it very clear to him that it was God who was speaking with him. The Lord gave Paul a number of visions. He received a vision on the Damascus road, another in the city of Damascus, and then the one he mentioned in our text (Acts 22:17). The Lord personally appeared to Paul in the vision in Jerusalem; he had earlier appeared to him on the Damascus road. The Jerusalem appearance took place in the very city that Paul had earlier set out from to persecute the Christians in Damascus. When Paul came back to Jerusalem, he returned a

---

[59] McReynolds, 1183, 1519.
[60] Stott, 348.

different man. He left the city with the purpose of persecuting Christians; he came back a believer in Jesus.

This new believer in Jesus had a vision when he was in the Temple. You may recall from chapter 8 that Zechariah, the priest, also had one there. While both men received their experiences in the Temple, they did not have them in the same location. Zechariah was a priest; as such, he had access to an area of the Temple that Paul would not have been permitted into. This is because Paul, though Jewish, was not a part of the priestly tribe; he was from the tribe of Benjamin (Phil. 3:5). Another characteristic these two visions share in common is that they were both received when prayer was taking place (Luke 1:8-13; Acts 22:17). One marked difference between the two visions was that Zechariah saw the angel Gabriel when he had his encounter, but Paul saw the Lord.

In his vision, the Lord told Paul to leave the city of Jerusalem. In fact, he was told twice to leave the city (Acts 22:18, 21). There was urgency in the Lord's message to him. This urgency can be seen in the use of the words "quick" and "immediately" (Acts 22:18). Paul was told to take prompt action. The Lord does not always tell his people why they should do certain things; he does not always explain himself. His command alone should be enough to compel obedience. However, in this case, the Lord did tell Paul why he was to leave: the people in Jerusalem would not accept his testimony about Jesus. Paul had something to say about this; he did not want to leave. After his brief comment in Acts 22:19-20, the Lord then gave him further instructions: he was told to go far away from Jerusalem because the Lord was sending him to the Gentiles. This directive is in keeping with what the Lord had said to him in an earlier vision; in Acts 26:17, he was told that he would be sent to the Gentiles.[61] The message in the Jerusalem vision redirected Paul and led him to make a geographic move. In addition to this, his ministry focus was also redirected; he was told that God was sending him to the Gentiles. His later ministry in Acts shows that he continued to reach out to Jewish people, but his major field of service became the Gentiles. Most Jewish believers in Jesus in Paul's time would probably not have liked

---

[61] Stott, 348.

the assignment he received!

Insights

One of the truths we can glean from this vision is that if we are in "the wrong place" the Lord can speak to us to reposition us in the right place. That is, if we are in a place where our ministry or testimony about Jesus is not going to be received, the Lord can speak to us and have us move on, rather than have us use our time and efforts in a place where we are not going to be productive. The Lord can use a vision to redirect us to a different location. This new location may be a different street, city, or state; it could even be a different country. He can also redirect us to a particular people group. The Lord of the harvest knows the fields. He also knows who will be effective in which location, and so he deploys his workers accordingly. The Lord's message to Paul was basically, "I have somewhere else for you to be." This was because there were many people who needed to hear about Jesus. If Paul had not heeded the Lord's word to him, many Gentiles may never have found their way to Jesus Christ. Paul's obedience led to the preaching of the gospel and the planting of churches in many predominantly Gentile areas.

An Afternoon Visitor

...he had a vision. (Acts 10:3)

In this chapter, we are studying a vision that took place in Caesarea. Caesarea was a garrison city which was named after Augustus Caesar; it was the administrative capital of Judea.[62] The recipient of this encounter was a military man named Cornelius. The text tells us that Cornelius was a centurion; a centurion was a soldier who commanded a unit of about 80 men.[63] Centurions, for the most part, were "soldiers who worked their way up through the ranks."[64] The mention of Cornelius' job is a secondary detail in the account. What is of primary importance is that he and his household were Gentiles (Acts 10:45).

Acts chapters 10, 11, and 15 make it clear that there was considerable concern, and discussion, in the early church about the place of Gentiles in the Christian community. A significant question arose about them. On what terms were they saved? Did they have to be circumcised and keep the Law of Moses, or was grace alone enough? Those who espoused circumcision and the keeping of the Law, and those who advocated a position of grace apart from works were both represented at the Jerusalem Council in Acts 15, and each side argued its case. The two opposing views are found in Acts 15:1, 5 and Acts 15:10-11.

Without knowing it or seeking it, Cornelius became a key player in helping the church define its doctrine. The vision he received set in motion a series of events that would have a great impact on Christian history. The events that took place in this religious man's house proved to be highly significant.

Acts 10:2 tells us about Cornelius' religious life: "He and all of his family

---

[62] Stott, 184-185.
[63] Keener, *Background*, 350.
[64] Ibid.

were devout and God-fearing." The fact that they are described as "God-fearing" may mean that they were non-Jews who had accepted the monotheism of the Jews and their ethical standards.[65] However, as Craig Keener says, "Cornelius is clearly not yet a full convert to Judaism (Acts 10:28)."[66] Acts 10:2 also provides us with some specifics about Cornelius' spiritual life; we learn that he maintained a regular prayer life and gave generously to people who were in need. He was fervent in the practice of his faith. His faith included both private and public dimensions; it was spiritual and practical; he ministered to the Lord and to people. In spite of his religious zeal, he was not saved (Acts 11:14). However, he received a vision, which would change his life and the lives of others.

Acts 10:3 tells us that Cornelius had a vision at three in the afternoon. This was one of the set times of prayer for the Jews, and it was the time of the evening offering (see Acts 3:1).[67] As has been the case with some of the other visions we have studied, Cornelius' vision involved an angel. An unnamed angel appeared to him (Acts 10:3). Accounts of his meeting with the angel are found in Acts 10:3-6, Acts 10:30-32, and Acts 11:13-14. In the initial account of the vision in Acts 10:3-6, the writer of Acts tells us about Cornelius' experience. The second account in Acts 10:30-32 is told from Cornelius' own lips as he recounts the events to Peter and the six men who had accompanied him (Acts 11:12). In the third account, in Acts 11:13-14, Peter relays the story to some Jewish brethren in Jerusalem, who were questioning his actions in going to a house of uncircumcised men and eating with them (Acts 11:3). We turn our attention now to the details of the vision.

This vision, like the others we have studied, has both visual and audible elements in it; Cornelius both saw and heard the angel. In fact, we are told he "distinctly" saw the angel (Acts 10:3). Unlike Saul's vision in Damascus (Acts 9:12), which he saw in his mind's eye (because he was physically blind when he received it), Cornelius saw the vision he received with his own eyes. He had it during the daytime when he was awake. The vision was very real

---

[65] Stott, 185.
[66] Keener, *Background*, 350.
[67] Ibid.

to him; it was both clear and vivid. The angel who spoke to him called him by name (Acts 10:3). Cornelius responded by asking the speaker what he wanted (Acts 10:4); then the angel delivered a message to him (Acts 10:4-5).

The message he received was two-fold; he was assured that his religious piety, that is, his prayers and gifts to the needy, had not escaped God's notice, and he was given instructions about what he should do. Cornelius was told to send for a man named Simon, who was also called Peter (Acts 10:5). He was also told where the man could be found. The instructions the angel gave him were detailed; first, he was told to send men to Joppa, which was a large town.[68] It was located about 30 miles away from Caesarea.[69] Then, even more specifically, Cornelius was told the house where this man would be. Peter could be found in the house of Simon the tanner, whose house was by the sea (Acts 9:6). Cornelius promptly obeyed the instructions he received in the vision.

The two passages in Acts 10 in which we are told the details of Cornelius' vision, Acts 10:3-6 and Acts 10:30-32, basically convey the same information. Acts 10:33 indicates that Cornelius knew he had been directed to send for Peter because Peter had a message from God to share with him. He may have surmised this because the angel had told him to contact Peter. However, there is additional biblical evidence to support the idea that more was said about the purpose of getting the two men together. There was definitely a divine purpose in it. In Acts 11, the apostle Peter recounted the events that had taken place at Cornelius' house to some of the Jews in Jerusalem. In Acts 11:14, Peter specifically said that the angel told Cornelius that Peter would bring a message to him by which he and his household would be saved. Some practicing religious people might have been offended at the suggestion that they were not already saved, and they might not have sent for Peter. However, if, as here, the message was delivered by an angel, a person might be a bit more cautious about dismissing it! Cornelius was not offended; he was receptive to what the angel said to him, and so he sent for Peter. Cornelius was so sure that Peter was going to come to his house and

---

[68] Keener, *Background*, 351.
[69] Ibid.

do what the angel had told him that he gathered other people together to hear what Peter was going to say (Acts 11:14). He had his relatives and close friends come to his house (Acts 10:24). That is faith!

Insights

We have studied a number of visions. In some of them, an angel appeared; in others, it was Jesus; and in one, another man appeared (Acts 9:12). In spite of these differences, all of the visions have been divinely-inspired. They have been given to different individuals or groups. Each vision has had a purpose for the person(s) involved. The purposes have included supplying information, giving direction, and calling a person into Christian service.

Up to this point in our study, all of those who received visions have been Jews. Cornelius is the first Gentile we have come to who received a vision, although he was one who was apparently trying to follow the God of Israel. Cornelius' experience demonstrates that God is not a respecter of ethnicity in the matter of giving visions. While he is certainly the God of the Jewish people, he is also the God of the Gentiles. In fact, he is the only God, and he truly cares for all the people of the world (John 3:16; Matt. 28:18-20).

This is also the first vision we have studied that was given specifically to bring people to salvation. Cornelius' vision shows us the lengths to which the Lord will go in order to bring a person to himself. God will use extraordinary means to bring a person to salvation. The Lord is currently doing this among Muslims, as I mentioned in the introduction of the book. This should encourage us. If we have friends or relatives that we think will never come to the Lord unless they have a highly supernatural experience, they just might have it! Biblical and current history demonstrates that the Lord can provide such experiences. Cornelius' experience helped provide acceptance for Gentiles in the Christian community, which includes many, if not most of you, who are reading this book. His obedience to the vision was crucial in bringing this about.

A Troubling Scene

...I saw a vision. (Acts 11:5)

The original account of Peter's vision is found in Acts 10. In that passage, we are told Peter "fell into a trance" and that heaven was opened (Acts 10:10-11). After that, we are told what he saw while he was in the trance (Acts 10:12). In the account in Acts 10 Peter's experience is not referred to as a vision; it was only later when Peter recounted what happened to some Jews in Jerusalem that he used the word "vision" to describe it (Acts 11:5). He said that while he was in a trance he saw the vision. So a vision was part of his subjective, supernatural experience. His vision is particularly interesting. This is because it contains a quality that we have not seen in the visions that we have studied so far. We will get to that shortly.

Peter's vision, like one that Paul had earlier (Acts 26:13), took place at about noontime (Acts 10:9). He received it while he was outside on the roof of a house in the city of Joppa. Specifically, he was on the roof of the house of Simon the tanner, which was located by the sea (Acts 10:6). At the time Peter had his vision, the messengers Cornelius sent were already on their way to get him in order to bring him back to Cornelius' house. This was not Peter's first visionary experience; he had one earlier when he was with James and John on the Mount of Transfiguration. A record of that vision is found in Matthew 17. At that time the three apostles saw Jesus transfigured before them. That vision took place prior to Jesus' crucifixion and resurrection. As far as we know, the vision we are studying in this chapter is the first, and only, vision that Peter received after Jesus' crucifixion and resurrection.

The vision came unannounced at a time when Peter was giving himself to prayer (Acts 10:9). The Bible does not give us any indication that he was seeking such an experience at that time; he was seeking the Lord. In fact, we can say quite confidently that if he had been seeking a vision, he would not have been seeking *this* vision. The biblical text makes it quite clear that Peter did not like what he saw or heard (Acts 10:14). Both the visual and audible aspects of this encounter were disturbing to his Jewish scruples. The instructions he received in the vision told him to eat things that were not proper for a Jewish person to eat, for the animals were "unclean" (Acts 10:14). Being told to eat the unclean animals was disturbing enough, but the Lord continued to press the issue with Peter three times (Acts 10:16)!

The Lord's persistence in this matter was probably due to Peter's repeated rejection of what God was saying to him in the vision. The Lord was not going to let his message be put aside. The Lord has a way of coming back to us again and again if we do not "get it" the first time. Peter was not the first person to initially resist what he was told in a vision. In chapter 12, we saw that Ananias, at first, resisted what the Lord had told him to do (Acts 9:13-14). However, Peter is the first person we have seen who has resisted the message of a vision more than once. Now we move on to the characteristic of this vision that distinguishes it from all of the other visions we have studied.

The thing that makes this vision interesting, indeed, unique in our study so far is that the meaning of the message of this vision was not immediately clear. Peter did not understand it at first, and the context makes clear the vision was not meant to be taken at face value. It contained symbols that needed to be interpreted. One example of this from the Old Testament is Daniel's vision in Daniel 7. The imagery in Peter's vision stood for something, and he had to try to figure out what it meant. Proof that interpretation was necessary can be found in Acts 10:17. In that verse, we are told that Peter was "wondering about the meaning of the vision." (The Lord does not always explain everything to us right away.) If Peter had understood what it meant, he would not have had to wonder about it. In this case, he could not immediately discern its meaning, so he reflected on it because its message was not clear to him. Two verses later, in Acts 10:19, we find he was still reflecting on the vision. Peter may have thought that God was testing him, and if that was the case, he certainly wanted to pass.[70] The

---

[70] Witherington, 350.

vision came at a time when he was hungry and he was told to eat unclean creatures, which good Jewish people did not eat. "Hungry he may be (10:10), but he is not *that* hungry."[71] So Peter puzzled over the meaning of the vision for a while.

Another thing which makes this vision interesting is that it complements the vision that had been given to Cornelius. This type of situation has been called "double vision."[72] The Lord directed Cornelius, through the vision of an angel, to send to Joppa for Peter, and in this vision the Lord was at work preparing Peter to leave Joppa to go to the home of Cornelius. God was working in the lives of two men, one a Jew and the other a Gentile, in order to bring them together. The trip that Peter was asked to make was definitely not one he had planned, but it was one that the Lord had planned. The Lord went to great lengths in order to make sure that these two men got together. Talk about divine appointments!

As Peter tried to discern the meaning of the vision, his thought processes were interrupted. Acts 10:19 tells us that the Holy Spirit spoke to him. Peter understood immediately what was said to him because the message was clear and direct; there was nothing that required interpretation. We must give Peter some credit here; he was sensitive and receptive to the Holy Spirit. We would all do well to follow his example in this. His spiritual sensitivity was probably born out of his previous experiences with the Spirit (Acts 2:4; 4:8, 31). The Holy Spirit was not a just a doctrine to Peter; he was a person with whom Peter was experientially familiar. The Spirit's words to him were the help he needed. He was told to go downstairs because there were three men who were looking for him (Acts 10:19-20). The admonition not to hesitate to go with the men seems to indicate that Peter might have had some reservations about going with them.

There are a few reasons why Peter might have balked at going with the three men. First, he very likely did not know them; they were probably strangers to him. Second, they initially outnumbered him; there were three of them (Acts 10:7, 19). Third, and most importantly, I think the main

---

[71] Keener, *Background*, 351.
[72] Ibid.

reason he might not have wanted to go with the men was because they were Gentiles. However, in spite of any concerns, he had the voice of the Spirit to overrule them.

Peter responded to the Spirit's message and went with the three men who had come to him from Cornelius' house. It is one thing to be open to the Holy Spirit and hear him; it is another to obey him: Peter did both. Here again, Peter is a good example for us to follow. When he arrived at Cornelius' house in Caesarea, Cornelius relayed to him the details of the vision he had received four days earlier (Acts 10:30-32). Acts 10:34b-35 tells us the lesson that Peter learned from all of this: "God does not show favoritism but accepts men from every nation who fear him and do what is right." The apostle then went on to preach to the large group of Gentiles who had gathered in Cornelius' house (Acts 10:27). He spoke to them about Jesus (Acts 10:36-43). This resulted in the Gentiles being saved and baptized with the Holy Spirit.

The visions of Cornelius and Peter were key factors in bringing about the glorious events that took place in the centurion's house. The gospel broke through ethnic barriers. The circumstances were orchestrated and confirmed by God (Acts 10:1-6; 9-23; 45-48; 11:5-18).

Insights

Peter's experience provides us with some additional insights about visions. First, not all visions are immediately understandable; some contain symbols that need to be interpreted in order for the meaning to become clear. There are times when God wants us to think about the symbols in order to discern the meaning of the vision. The story of Peter also shows us that sometimes we need help in order to discern the meaning of a vision. The intervention of the Holy Spirit helped move Peter toward an understanding of what the Lord was saying to him. The Lord knows when we need help to understand what he is saying to us. This is perhaps especially true when the message we have been given is in symbolic form or when the vision concerns a lesson we have not yet fully grasped.

A second thing we can learn from this vision is that, if necessary, the

Lord will repeatedly press his message so that the person receiving it will face it and seek out its meaning. He did this to Peter with this vision of the sheet that had unclean animals in it. Peter's vision took him out of his comfort zone. Though this stretched him a bit, it resulted in him being brought more in line with God's will. The Lord will sometimes do that with his people today as well.

Finally, this vision shows us that God can communicate with his people during times of prayer. Peter had the vision while he was setting himself apart to pray (Zechariah and Paul also received visions during times of prayer—see Luke 1:10, 13 and Acts 9:11-12). Peter's vision was not technically predictive in nature; however, it did prepare Peter for a challenge he was about to face in his ministry. Even experienced ministers can have hang-ups and blind spots, but the Lord can help them overcome these things so that they can serve his greater purposes. Visions are one of the means he uses to accomplish this.

Getting on Track

...Paul had a vision of a man of Macedonia. (Acts 16:9)

The vision that we are studying in this chapter took place in Troas when Paul and his companions Silas, Timothy, and Luke were there. This team had not been together very long. Paul had previously worked with Silas (Acts 15:25-27), but the other members of the team did not join him until the start of the missionary journey that began in Acts 16. Prior to this journey Paul had a disagreement with his former traveling companion, Barnabas. The two men were at odds about whether John Mark should accompany them on their next journey. Their disagreement was so severe that the two men parted company (Acts 15:37-39). Barnabas took John Mark and went to Cyprus (Acts 15:39). Paul then chose Silas to travel with him (Acts 15:40). Timothy was added to the team a short time later (Acts 16:1-3). We do not know how, or when, Luke joined the team. He is not mentioned in Acts 16, but there is evidence that he was present. Tradition tells us that Luke was the author of Acts.[73] In Acts 16:10, the author of Acts says, "we"; in doing so, he indicates that he was with the other men, so he was present at the time.[74]

This team was quite a collection of men. In my earlier book, *Apostles, Prophets, Evangelists, Pastors, and Teachers Then and Now*, I pointed out that some of these men functioned in more than one ministry. Paul was an apostle (Gal. 1:1; Eph. 1:1), who would later also refer to himself as a teacher (2 Tim. 1:11).[75] Silas was a prophet (Acts 15:32), whom Paul would later identify also as an apostle (1 Thess. 1:1 and 2:6).[76] Timothy was later

---

[73] Keener, *Background*, 320.
[74] Ibid., 367.
[75] John P. Lathrop, *Apostles, Prophets, Evangelists, Pastors, and Teachers Then and Now* (Maitland, FL: Xulon Press, 2008), 37.
[76] Ibid., 50.

referred to by Paul as an apostle (1 Thess. 1:1 and 2:6).[77] He also seems to have been a teacher (1 Tim. 4:13).[78] In fact, I think it is safe to say that all who were apostles were also teachers.[79] Paul also encouraged Timothy to do the work of an evangelist (2 Tim. 4:5). These were men of significant spiritual caliber and giftedness; they were leaders in the church (Eph. 4:11). However, in spite of all their spirituality, they encountered some opposition on this missionary journey.

Opposition is to be expected in ministry. Jesus encountered it (Matt. 21:45-46; John 1:10-11; 2:18), and he told his followers that they would also experience it (Matt. 10:17-22). Biblical history shows that Jesus was right; persecution was regularly encountered by the church (Acts 4:1-3, 18-21; 5:17-18, 40; 8:1-3; 12:1-3; 16:22-24).

However, the opposition that Paul and his companions encountered did not come from the places we might expect; it did not come from the devil or from people. The Bible tells us that the Lord hindered them from entering certain fields of ministry. Acts 16:6 tells us that the Holy Spirit kept the team from preaching the word in Asia. The very next verse, Acts 16:7, tells us that the Spirit of Jesus would not allow them to enter Bithynia. We are not given the details of how the Spirit kept them out of these areas, nor are we told how they knew God was the one who was preventing them from entering these places. We also do not know whether they realized the Lord was hindering them at the time the events took place, or later when they looked back and saw what had taken place as a result of their redirection. One thing we can say about this ministry team is that they were persistent! Persistence is a quality that is essential for any type of ministry.

The closed doors the missionaries encountered eventually brought them to Troas. Troas was a city located near the Aegean Sea.[80] The vision, which Paul received, was given at a time when the men were actively seeking to minister for the Lord. This vision is one which might also be considered a

---

[77] Ibid., 37.
[78] Keener, *Background*, 615.
[79] Lathrop, 81.
[80] Walvoord and Zuck, 398.

dream.[81] This is because the text tells us Paul had this vision at night. The Bible does not tell us whether Paul was asleep or awake when he received this revelation. If he was awake when he received it, it would be a vision. If he was asleep, it would be a dream. I do not think this is a major issue. Whether it was a vision or a dream, it was still a revelation from the Lord. I am considering it as a vision because the word "vision" is used in the text.

The vision came at an important time. The missionary team seemed to have hit a wall in their Christian service. Their ministry plans were being thwarted; they had been kept out of both Asia and Bithynia. It must have been frustrating to encounter the closed doors (Rev. 3:7). They had invested both time and energy trying to go to these places to minister. I take great comfort in this passage because this group of ministers, who were without question spiritual men, seems, at this point, to be operating by trial and error. They try one field of service, and it doesn't work, so they move on to another. If the truth be told, many times in the church today we operate this way. The men in our text were not certain where they should be, but they are actively trying to find out, and that is to be commended. They were in some sense experiencing negative guidance.[82] The Lord used the closed doors to keep them from engaging in ministry in places that they should not be at that time.

After the negative guidance, the Lord provided the team with some positive guidance.[83] This guidance did not come amidst the activities of the day, but rather at night, at a time when the men would be settling in. One of the men, Paul, had a vision in the night of a man of Macedonia begging him, "Come over to Macedonia and help us" (Acts 16:9). There was urgency in the words; the man was begging Paul to come to Macedonia. Paul shared this vision with the rest of his coworkers. Acts 16:10 tells us that the team reached the conclusion that the Lord was calling them to go to Macedonia. So, off they went.

It is interesting to note that in this vision, while unusual or cryptic

---

[81] Stott, 260.
[82] Ibid.
[83] Ibid.

images (like the unclean animals Peter saw in the sheet in Acts 10) were not used, the men still had to determine what God was saying to them. In the vision Paul did not receive a direct order to go into Macedonia; the team had to interpret the vision in order to get the message that the Lord was giving them. They had to interpret what "help" meant (Acts 16:9). Acts 16:10 tells us they concluded that the vision meant they were to preach the gospel to the people in Macedonia. This vision should be of particular interest to Christians in the West because as a result of it the gospel was brought to Europe and subsequently to North America.[84]

Insights

We can learn from our text that the Lord may guide us through a vision when we are in need of direction and guidance. He can, of course, guide us through other means, but since he can use visions, we should remain open to that possibility as well.

A second lesson we recognize from this passage is that the Lord can give one person a vision in order to guide a group of people. We see that in Acts 16. Paul received a vision, but the whole group was given guidance through it. Since this is so, we need to embrace receiving the ministries of other Christians, because the Lord, will, at times use them to guide us in the work of the Kingdom.

Paul's experience also shows us that sometimes group discernment or interpretation is appropriate in understanding the meaning of a vision. It is also a safeguard; it can help keep an individual or the group on the right path. If a group of believers agrees about the meaning of a subjective experience, like a vision, then the likelihood of wrong interpretation is diminished.

In closing this chapter, we see that this vision shows us the Lord's care for the nations. He directed the missionaries into the area that we now know as Europe. From Europe the gospel was carried to "Africa, Asia, North America, Latin America and Oceania."[85] "May the nations be glad and sing

---

[84] Ibid., 258.
[85] Ibid.

for joy, for you rule the peoples justly and guide the nations of the earth. Selah. May the peoples praise you, O God; may all the peoples praise you" (Ps. 67:4-5).

Stay Put

One night the Lord spoke to Paul in a vision... (Acts 18:9)

O ur study up to this point has shown that the apostle Paul had a number of visions. He had one which brought him to believe in Jesus and launched him into gospel ministry (Acts 26:12-19), one which assured him that his sight would be restored (Acts 9:12), one which told him to leave Jerusalem (Acts 22:17-18), and one which gave him and his companions the direction they needed to find the field of ministry the Lord wanted them to go to (Acts 16:9). Visions seem to follow Paul. In this chapter we will be looking at yet another vision that Paul received.

The vision that we are studying in this chapter took place in Corinth (Acts 18:1, 9). This city was located in Achaia. Paul spent a year and a half there (Acts 18:11) and planted a church. A brief look at a Bible map will show that the locations where Paul received his visions were many miles apart. Paul received visions not just in different cities but in different countries. Interestingly enough, none of Paul's visions that we have details for, took place in the land of Israel. I don't think that there is any deep religious significance to this; it was probably just because Paul spent the majority of his time in ministry outside of the land of Israel. He was the apostle to the Gentiles (Rom. 11:13; Gal. 2:8), and so he spent considerable time ministering in the lands where they lived.

In Paul's day, Corinth was a major urban center.[86] The city was very diverse culturally and was known for its prosperity and sexual immorality.[87] Paul's companions, Silas and Timothy, were with him in Corinth (Acts 18:5), but the biblical text focuses on Paul and his activities in the city.

In Corinth, as in other places, the preaching of the gospel met with opposition, this time the opposition came from people. Following a pattern

---

[86] Keener, *Background*, 451.
[87] Ibid.

that can be seen earlier in Acts, the chief opposition to the gospel in Corinth came from the Jewish community.[88] We can see evidence of this opposition a couple of times in Paul's ministry in Corinth (Acts 18:6, 12). He reached out to the Jews and Greeks in the synagogue (Acts 18:4) with the news that their Messiah had come. Many of the Jews did not welcome his message. On the contrary, we are told that they "opposed Paul and became abusive" (Acts 18:6). They were hostile to both the message and the messenger. Paul told his opponents that their blood was on their own heads and that he would now turn his attention to the Gentiles (Acts 18:6). When he spoke of their blood being on their own heads, "he was referring to their destruction and their own responsibility for it (cf. Ezek. 33:1-6)."[89] This statement, coupled with his remark that he would then direct his ministry to the Gentiles, surely did not win him any friends from the Jews who were opposing him. Jewish resistance to the gospel and Paul's turning to reach out to the Gentiles is a recurring pattern in Acts.[90]

The conflict that ensued was so great that Paul left the synagogue where he had been speaking. He did not go very far; we are told that he went next door to the house of a worshipper of God named Titius Justus (Acts 18:7). After this, we are given a brief, one-verse report that tells us some of the people who accepted the gospel message in Corinth. Crispus, the ruler of the synagogue, and his whole household came to believe in the Lord (the word "Lord" here is surely a reference to Jesus since the Jews already believed in the God of Israel). In addition to him and his household, we are told that there were many others in Corinth who became believers in Jesus, though we are not given any of their names. The response to the gospel in Corinth was mixed; there were those who rejected it and those who accepted it.

In the midst of these bittersweet circumstances the Lord spoke to Paul in a vision. Like the one he had in Acts 16, this one took place at night. Because it was a night vision, it is possible that this experience may have

---

[88] Walvoord and Zuck, 405.

[89] Ibid., 407.

[90] Ibid., 405.

been a dream.[91] Ancient peoples regularly used the words "dream" and "vision" freely to describe the same experience; they used the words "interchangeably."[92] However, once again I am including Paul's experience in the vision section of the book because that is what the biblical text calls it (Acts 18:9).

In this vision the Lord told Paul not to hold back on his ministry, "keep speaking, do not be silent" (Acts 18:9). In essence, he was told "stay put, and keep on doing what you are doing." This indicates the Lord's approval of his work in the city, in spite of the some of the Jews opposition to it. The Lord also assured him that he was not going to be hurt (Acts 18:10). In response to this revelation, Paul stayed in Corinth for a year and a half (Acts 18:11). The revelation that he was not going to be harmed must have given Paul confidence; it was a word of encouragement. He had already suffered opposition in the city, and Acts 18:12-16 makes it clear that he later encountered additional trouble there.

Insights

The vision Paul received in Acts 18, like some of his previous visions, contained a prophetic element; that is, in a very general way, it foretold the future. Paul was told that no one would attack and harm him (Acts 18:10). The Lord encouraged Paul by letting him know something that he could not know through natural means. In fact, I doubt Paul would have thought this at all, based on the events that had transpired just prior to the vision. There were definitely people in the city who were hostile to him. The Lord can also speak to his people today and let them know that they are going to be protected in their labors for him. This would be a particular blessing to those who serve in lands which are hostile to the gospel message.

The thing that I find most interesting about this revelation is that it is a vision "to stay." Paul was told to continue doing ministry in Corinth. His response to the vision, recorded in Acts 18:11, indicates that he understood this. We may be tempted to think that the primary purpose of visions is to

---

[91] Ryken and Wilhoit, et al., s. v. "Dreams, Visions," 217.
[92] Ibid.

redirect us to other places of service (as in Acts 16:6-10). That is one purpose, but it is not the only one. Paul's divine encounter in Corinth shows us that the Lord can give a person a vision so that they will "stay where they are." The Lord is vitally concerned that we be in the right place, the place he wants us to be. The problem, of course, is that sometimes the right place doesn't look like the right place to us. Hostility and opposition can, at times, color our perception of the will of God. The Lord does not want us to abandon a field of ministry just because we encounter opposition. We might be in the beginning stages of a ministry which will turn out to be very fruitful. If circumstances might tempt us to move on, the Lord can intervene and let us know that he wants us to stay right where we are. The fact that trouble erupts does not mean that we are not in right place; we may be exactly where God wants us to be. If we are in the right place, then the Lord will provide what we need in order to stay to complete the work he has given us to do.

Additional References

In this chapter we will be looking at some additional references to visions in the New Testament. Three of the references are found in Acts, and the remainder comes from 2 Corinthians and Revelation. I will begin with the texts in 2 Corinthians and Revelation and then return to the ones in Acts. My comments about these texts will be very brief.

The first reference that we will consider is 2 Corinthians 12:1. In this text Paul mentions visions and revelations from the Lord. Both words are in the plural, meaning that there were a number of them. Paul said he knew a man who had these. Some believe that the person Paul was speaking about in this text was himself.[93] The larger context seems to support this interpretation. After mentioning visions and revelations from the Lord (2 Cor. 12:1), Paul goes on to say that because of the greatness of the revelations he was given "a thorn in the flesh, a messenger of Satan" (2 Cor. 12:7). He would not need this thorn if he did not have great revelations.[94] The personal reference seems to confirm that he was speaking about himself.

Paul does not give us a lot of information about these visions and revelations, and he tells us the reason why. He did not share the things he experienced because he saw things "man is not permitted to tell" (2 Cor. 12:4). The only thing he does tell us is that they took place in the third heaven or paradise (2 Cor. 12:2, 4). The third heaven, in Paul's thinking, was probably the highest heaven, the place where paradise is located.[95]

The next reference we will look at comes from the book of Revelation. In Revelation 9, the apostle John wrote about what he saw as the trumpet

---

[93] Walvoord and Zuck, 582.
[94] Craig S. Keener, *1-2 Corinthians*, The New Cambridge Bible Commentary (New York, NY: Cambridge University Press, 2005), 238.
[95] Keener, *Background*, 514.

judgments were taking place. The New International Version translation of Revelation 9:17 is the only place in the book where the translators have used the word "vision" to describe what John saw.

In the opening chapter of Revelation, John, the writer of the book, refers to it as a book of prophecy (Rev. 1:3). This is certainly true for two reasons. First, the writer of the book says that it is prophecy and he wrote under the inspiration of the Holy Spirit. Second, the book of Revelation contains a significant amount of material that is predictive in nature. However, that being said, I do not think it can be denied that much of Revelation is a vision. Some of what John saw was "otherworldly," things such as the living creatures (Rev. 4:6-8), the dragon (Rev. 12:3), and the beasts (Rev. 13:1-2; 11). In addition, some of what John saw had not *actually* taken place at the time he saw it. The events had not yet played out in human history. In fact, there are things that are still yet to come.

There is one other verse in Revelation that contains a Greek word that is sometimes translated as "vision." The text is Revelation 4:3 where the word *horasis* appears twice.[96] I have consulted a number of Bible translations, and none of them translates *horasis* as "vision" in this verse. Instead, in Revelation 4:3, the word is used to describe how the one on the throne and the rainbow looked. Since there seems to be a different shade of meaning, indicated by the translation of the word in this verse, I am not treating this verse at length in this study.

We turn our attention now to the texts in Acts. The first one is found in Acts 7:31. This verse was part of Stephen's address to the Sanhedrin. The text refers to an angel's appearance to Moses; this actually took place back in Exodus 3. One of the Greek words that is translated as "vision" is used in Acts 7:31.[97] However, in this instance it seems to have a different shade of meaning, and a number of Bible translations that I have consulted do not refer to this experience as a vision. Also, this event did not actually take place during the New Testament time period, so I will not be treating it in this study.

---

[96] McReynolds, 1519.
[97] Ibid.

The next Acts text I want to discuss that has the word "vision" in it is Acts 12:9. In this verse we are told that the apostle Peter thought he was seeing a vision when an angel helped him escape from prison. The rest of the verse reveals that Peter's thought was incorrect. He was not seeing a vision; what he was seeing was actually taking place.

The last Acts reference that I want to call your attention to actually appears before the other two that we have looked at in this chapter. This reference is Acts 2:17. I have a reason for mentioning this text last.

In Acts 2:17, Peter was preaching in the Jewish capital, the city of Jerusalem, on the Feast of Pentecost. As he began his sermon, he addressed the charge that some people were making about the disciples. Some in the crowd said that the disciples of Jesus had had too much wine to drink. In other words, they were accusing the disciples of being drunk. Peter said that this was not the case, and he then went on to give them the proper explanation for what was happening. He told the people that what had taken place was what the prophet Joel had predicted (Acts 2:16-21); the Holy Spirit was being poured out. Joel's prophecy associated three kinds of divine communication with the outpouring of the Spirit; specifically, it mentioned prophecy, dreams, and visions.

I saved the consideration of Acts 2:17 until last because it is in some sense "a promise of more to come." The supernatural communications that Peter mentioned in his sermon are to take place in the last days. As I mentioned in the introduction of the book, biblically speaking, the last days began in Christ.[98] They will continue until the last day (John 6:39). The continuing nature of these phenomena can be witnessed in the life of the New Testament church. The book of Acts contains a number of references to dreams, visions, and prophecy. This shows us that the outpouring of the Holy Spirit was not a one-time event. When we move to part three of this book, we will see that dreams and visions have continued on and are still happening in today's world. This should not surprise us. The Lord is the same yesterday, today, and forever (Heb. 13:8). Also, we are living in the time period when God said that prophecy, dreams, and visions would take

---

[98] Keener, *Background*, 651.

place.

Insights

Let me summarize what we can learn from these various texts. The text of 2 Corinthians 12:1, at least by implication, teaches us that there are some things God may reveal to us that are not for us to share with other people. Paul would not reveal to others the things that God revealed to him in the third heaven. While we might be tempted to impress others by sharing with them the things God reveals to us, that does not mean that we should always do so. There are some things that God reveals to an individual that are only for that person to know.

The visions in the book of Revelation show us that God can reveal things of worldwide significance to one of his servants, things that affect nations. Revelation also shows us that God can reveal things to his people that they will never see take place during their lifetime. This was certainly true of the Old Testament prophets who wrote about the coming Messiah (1 Pet. 1:10-12); it was also true of the apostle John. He did not see in the natural all that he saw in the Spirit.

Acts 2:17, coupled with the history recorded in the rest of the book, shows us that the outpouring of the Holy Spirit in the last days makes visions, as well as dreams and prophecy, available to more people. We should expect to find them in our day. Before moving on to accounts of modern-day dreams and visions, we need to take a brief look at some difficult passages; we will do that in the next chapter.

Difficult Passages

In the first two parts of this book, we studied the dreams and visions found in the New Testament. We looked at texts that were clearly identified as dreams or visions. The texts contained the word "dream" or "vision" in them, either in English or in New Testament Greek (as in Matthew 17:9). The one exception to this was Acts 22:17 which made reference to a trance. I included this account in the visions section because of Peter's experience in Acts 10; he was in a trance (Acts 10:10) and saw a vision (Acts 10:17). There seems to be some connection between trances and visions. Paul's experience in Acts 22 also had other characteristics that we found in visions, namely, that there were audible and visual elements involved in the experience.

In all of the cases we have examined, the recipient was aware of something that was not a regular part of life as we know it. At times we encountered passages in which a particular experience could be either a dream or a vision. This was the case in passages where a person had a vision at night. In those cases I made a judgment call and considered them visions because the biblical texts referred to them as visions.

As I was nearing the end of my study of the biblical material, I found that there were some texts that one writer considered to be a dream and another considered to be a vision. Acts 23:11 and Acts 27:23-24 are two such cases. In Acts 23:11 we are told that the Lord stood near Paul one night and spoke to him. In Acts 27:23-24 we learn that an angel of God stood near Paul and spoke to him when he was on a ship. The problem, however, is that the words "dream" and "vision" are not mentioned in connection with either of these events.

These two texts raised a question: Was it always a dream or vision when the Lord or an angel (or in some cases another man) appeared to a person in the New Testament? This seemed to be the case quite frequently, but I was not sure that this was true in all cases. Without having researched it further, I raised this issue with a friend in an email. In his response, he reminded me of other texts in which there were supernatural visitations that are not called either dreams or visions. He mentioned the angel Gabriel's visit to Mary in Luke 1, and the angels' appearance to the shepherds in Luke 2. So the number of these "problem texts" was growing. They did not fit nicely into my theological categories as I had hoped. What was I to do with them? Were they dreams or visions or were they something else?

One day as I was reading in the book of Acts, my mind wandered ahead to Acts 12. In that chapter we find the account of Peter's escape from prison. In the midst of the story I found a very helpful piece of information. Acts 12:9 tells us that as Peter was being led out of prison by the angel, "he thought he was seeing a vision." However, the first part of the verse tells us that "what the angel was doing *was really happening*" (emphasis mine). This seems to indicate that there is a difference between a vision (or dream) and reality. Based on this insight, I have not classified the texts mentioned in this section as either dreams or visions, and I have not devoted a chapter to studying each.

Part Three

Dreams & Visions
in Modern Times

Dreams

U p to this point in our study of dreams, we have given most of our attention to biblical texts; this has been essential in laying the groundwork for the study. Examining Scripture has helped us gain some understanding of the ways that God works in dreams. But divinely-inspired dreams continued beyond the first century. The continuation of these God-given dreams was mentioned in the introduction of the book. The statements made in the "insights" section at the end of each chapter also affirm that divinely-inspired dreams are for today. Acts 2:17 in particular indicates that dreams will continue; they will take place in the period of time known as last days. I have referred to this text as "a promise of more to come." Dreams are connected with the outpouring of the Holy Spirit, which began on the day of Pentecost.

It is not my intent in this book to provide an extensive study of dreams in the Christian faith. If you are looking for information about how dreams were regarded in earlier church history, subsequent to the first century, you can consult chapter 6 of Morton Kelsey's book *Dreams: A Way to Listen to God*.[99] In this chapter, he notes the value early church leaders placed on dreams and mentions some of the dreams that certain individuals had.[100]

In this chapter we are going to focus on God-given dreams of the twentieth and twenty-first centuries. I am confident that the dreams you will find here came from God. I say this with confidence. The accuracy of the things that were revealed and the fruit that has resulted as people have acted on these dreams demonstrate that they were given by God.

Most of the testimonies in this chapter come from people I have

---

[99] Morton Kelsey, *Dreams: A Way to Listen to God* (New York: NY: Paulist Press, 1978), 71-77.
[100] Ibid.

personally met or from those I have made contact with through my network of friends. Toward the end of the chapter you may encounter a couple of names that are more familiar to you. However, they all share at least one thing in common: God spoke to them through a dream. Let us turn now to their stories.

"Jake"

"Jake" is a pseudonym; the true identity of this contributor is not being revealed for security reasons. The dreams he shared with me are not his own but those of people he has encountered in ministry. The identities of those he has written about are also withheld for security reasons. The dreams in this first section all resulted in people coming to faith in Jesus.

Dreams Leading to Salvation

"H's" Dream

> A short-term mission team shared the gospel with a man that we will call "H." The believers gave this man a Bible and told him to read the gospel of Mark. The next day when they met with him, he had read the gospels of Matthew, Mark, and Luke. He said that he loved what he had read but that the Koran doesn't teach the same thing, so the Bible must have been changed. The Christians told him that if he was really hungry to know the truth God would reveal it to him. By faith they told "H" that he would have a dream. That night he dreamed that God was inviting him into something great.

"M's" Dream

> I visited a 38-year-old man named "M." Two years earlier he had had a dream. In the dream he was on a sinking boat and about to drown. Suddenly a hand reached out to save him. He immediately knew it was Jesus. He couldn't see his face, but described him as shining like the sun. He woke up a

changed man and since that time has not had any doubt that
Jesus is Lord and Savior. He now wants to be baptized.

"Z's" Dream

A woman in her 40s that we will call "Z" had a dream that
the police came to her house. In fear she ran with her Bible
and Christian CDs to bury them in the ground. As she dug
she discovered a Bible in the ground. She then tried to dig in
another place, and as she dug she found another Bible in the
earth. This happened again and again, and finally she heard
a voice say, "This is your way." She woke up and gave her life
to Christ. She was the first in her family to be saved.

A few years later, after praying for her husband, who resisted
her new life, he had a dream. Her husband saw a calamity
and a mighty storm. In fear a crowd of thousands of people
all called on the name of Mohammed to deliver them, "Z's"
husband then lifted up his hand and cried out in the name of
Jesus; then he woke up. After he had this dream, he gave his
life to the Lord. Now, the entire family, including their three
children, are all believers in Jesus and are part of a church.

Ministry-Related Dreams

In this section we will be looking at dreams that provided leading or
guidance regarding ministry. The dreams that you will find below have
come from a number of different sources; like the dreams above, they are
also relatively recent, having taken place in the twentieth or twenty-first
centuries.

Eugene Smith

Eugene Smith is a minister from Canada who currently pastors the
Ballymena Elim Pentecostal Church in Ireland. He is heavily involved in
missions and has made many trips to Africa. Eugene is also the author of a

number of books that deal with biblical subjects including, *The Privilege of Prayer* (Vision Publishing, 2005), and *The Twelve Jesus Chose* (Vision Publishing, 2007). In an email dated February 27, 2012, he shared the following dream with me.

> When I was 16, I dreamed that the pastor of the church I was attending approached me and asked if I would like to preach! I enthusiastically said, "Yes!" When the pastor walked away, I saw myself sit at a desk with pen and paper and a Bible in front of me. I began to write out a sermon!

> When I awoke from this dream, I remembered the sermon! (How I wish that every message would come that easily!) My text was Matthew 22:29: "...Ye do err, not knowing the scriptures, nor the power of God" (KJV). The thrust of the message was simple enough: to be free from error, one must know both the scriptures and the power of God in the person of the Holy Spirit. It is not enough to be knowledgeable of the scriptures; one must also know the Holy Spirit. Neither is it right to know the Holy Spirit without deeply knowing the scriptures. God has never intended the believer to follow one or the other, the believer is to pursue both. The Word is not to function without the Spirit, and the Spirit does not work outside the boundaries of the Word. The two always go together.

> It was only many years later that I realized that this dream was God showing me the major emphasis he would lay upon my heart. I would develop a very strong burden that God's people would intimately know the scriptures, especially those who claim to be Spirit-filled. Spirit and Word must unite. This would be the main driving burden of my heart for years as I would travel and teach.

Constantine Murefu

Constantine Murefu and I were classmates in the early 1980s at Zion Bible Institute in East Providence, Rhode Island. He now holds a Ph.D. in philosophy and is very active in ministry which includes, among other things, serving as the President of Living Waters Bible Seminary in Harare, Zimbabwe. The accounts below come from an email he sent me on March 4, 2012.

His Mother's Dream

> Over 30 years ago my mother, Mrs. Agnes Murefu, who is now about 85 years old, had a dream about me and my brother. She saw us cycling up a mountain. My brother was ahead of me, and I caught up with him and overtook him. I then waited for him and helped him come up to where I was.
>
> She interpreted the dream to mean that we would have the same profession; I would go ahead of my brother and then help him to get to where I was. This has come true. My brother Titus responded to the call to ministry ahead of me; he went to Bible college and trained. Later on I responded, but my training took me beyond a diploma to a B.A. degree, then an M.A., and later a Ph.D. I then helped my brother to get his first degree, and go on to a M.A. Now he has two master's degrees and is currently studying for his doctorate. I helped him in these pursuits. He is currently the Deputy President of the Apostolic Faith Mission in Zimbabwe, and I am the International Deputy President of the Apostolic Faith Mission International.

Constantine's Dream

> I also had some dreams about getting on a plane in order to go study in a distant country. I saw the classroom setup and

the buildings in my dream. When I arrived at Zion Bible
Institute in 1980, it seemed like I had been there before. I
realized that two of the buildings I had seen in my dream
were the Gracemore Building and Zion Gospel Temple. I also
recognized one of the people I had seen in my dream as
Sister Messerlian. In fact, I had been there before, in a dream!

Nancy Hudson

Nancy Hudson is an American who has served as a missionary in South
Africa for over 20 years. She oversees a group of churches called Christian
Assemblies of South Africa (CASA). Part of her story is told in chapter 4 of
the book *Some Men Are Our Heroes: Stories by Women About the Men Who Have
Greatly Influenced Their Lives*.[101] The account below comes from an email she
sent me on January 2, 2012.

John and I had come from the mission ship, got married, and
started working with our church. We sought missions work
but kept getting rejected. I clearly had a dream in which I
entered a field and could see all sides of it. As I continued
walking, I entered another field where I could not see the end
of it. The field was filled with many rows of grapes, white and
black grapes. There were many workers in the field wearing
sun hats and picking the grapes. I came upon a large packing
shed where I met a large black man. I asked him where the
master of the field was. He said, "He is not here right now,
but he is returning soon, just help yourself while you wait."

I did not understand the dream. I later told the dream to a
woman, and she said, "Perhaps you will go to South Africa
where there are black and white people." I thought, *no, I don't*

---

[101] KeumJu Jewel Hyun and Cynthia Davis Lathrop, *Some Men are Our Heroes: Stories by
Women About the Men Who Have Greatly Influenced Their Lives* (Eugene, OR: Wipf &
Stock Publishers, 2010), 36-44.

think I would go to such a place. But, I did end up in South Africa, and there are packing sheds, like large open lean-to buildings where all the workers take what they pick. We worked at one ourselves, and I remembered the dream. We were just beginning our ministry. The main point of the dream is that there is a great harvest out there just ripe for picking.

"Marty"

"Marty" is a preacher; he has asked that his real name not be used. The account that follows is based on information he sent to me in an email.

In 2002, I was a youth pastor at a mainline Protestant church. I was pastoring a Spirit-filled youth group that had been growing because of the work of the Spirit in our midst. At that time, the thought of leaving this church was far from my mind because the ministry was doing really well.

One night I had a strange dream; a well-known pastor in my city appeared to me in the dream and said, "Pastors today need to leave by faith." I had no idea what God was trying to tell me. The pastor in the dream was part of the same Protestant denomination as I was, and he led a growing congregation.

The following year as the ministry team was praying, we suddenly had a sense that the enemy was going to strike our youth ministry. Warning after warning came from various pastors who crossed my path. Finally in June 2003, the dream and all the prophetic warnings we had received finally made sense. There was a change in leadership in the mainline denomination. The retiring leader was a Spirit-filled believer who allowed the churches to have charismatic expressions in the church services. However, the new leader was one who preferred traditions. Because of this, he wanted to remove me from my position in the local church. The dream finally made sense to me. The Lord used the pastor in the dream to speak to me. This pastor and his congregation also left the mainline denomination. As a leadership team, we felt that if the new leader of the mainline denomination could no longer tolerate differences in spiritual expression, it was time for us to leave. So in 2004, our leadership team told our church's pastor that we would be leaving the church with a group of young people who had decided to come out together with us. The pastor of our local church graciously released us, and we had a last church service together before we parted ways. It was interesting that God confirmed our decision to leave in a most amazing way.

On the day I tendered my resignation, I receive a call from a pastor informing me that the pastor I had seem in my dream wanted to meet me. This would be the first time that I would meet him; up to this point I knew of him but did not know him personally. He asked me why I left the mainline church. I told him what happened. At the end of our conversation, he affirmed to me that our decision was from the Lord, and he laid his hands upon me and blessed me. It is amazing to me that, after receiving a directive dream with this pastor in it whom I did not know personally, he later winds up praying for me and blessing me.

Because I had no desire to start a church of my own, I decided that we would join another church. The group that left with us became the youth ministry of this church.

Revival came in 2007; the Spirit of God fell strongly upon the young people. It started with a spirit of prayer and intercession. Young people were fervently praying and crying out to God to save their generation. Revival broke out in the youth camp we held that year. On the last day of the camp, we sent about 70 young people out into the streets challenging them to bring young people from the streets to the campsite. By the time they returned, they brought back a total of 160 youths. The gospel was preached, and that night we registered 32 first-time decisions for Jesus. Following this event that year we saw 200 decisions for Jesus Christ. It was certainly revival in the youth ministry; during the youth service the presence of God was very strong. At every youth service we had kids accepting Jesus. During that period, God would also at times pour out gold dust upon us; we noticed that our faces were glittering under the light. Very often in our services, because the presence of God was so strong, demons would manifest and we would cast them out. We never had a boring youth service at that time!

While revival was exciting, it was also painful. During the time all of these exciting things were happening, the senior pastor became very insecure and began attacking me and the ministry. The attacks became so bad that I became discouraged and burned out. I decided to resign. The youth ministry closed down not long after I left the church. Sadly, some backslid in their faith. However, many of my ex-leaders are still serving God faithfully in other churches. One of them has become the youth pastor of a thriving church, and many others are doing social work with Christian organizations.

R. Loren Sandford

R. Loren Sandford is the Senior Pastor of New Song Church and Ministries in Denver, Colorado. He is a widely recognized prophetic minister and has written a number of books dealing with the prophetic including: *The*

Prophetic Church: Wielding the Power to Change the World (Chosen, 2009), and most recently *Visions of the Coming Days: What to Look for and How to Prepare* (Chosen, 2012). In an email dated October 15, 2011, he shared the following dream with me.

> In 1990 I was struggling with whether or not I was being called to leave the church I had planted in North Idaho and pastored for 11 years to move to Denver to become the executive pastor of a large church there. It would mean leaving my role with Elijah House, my parents' ministry that I had helped develop, as well as all my siblings who lived in the area. In the midst of this, the Lord sent an angel in a dream. It came out of the sun in a blaze of golden light and handed me a Denver newspaper with an article about my coming. As I read the article, it turned out to be a letter to me from God. Each word caused a huge explosion of power that I felt in my chest. All I could remember upon waking was, "I am sending you to Denver to improve the flow of my Spirit." I obeyed, sold my home, uprooted my family, and moved. My sojourn at the church that called me didn't last long. In the end I planted a church in Denver that became a significant influence in bringing other churches into the flow of the Toronto Blessing that began in January 1994. The flow continues!

Jackie Pullinger

Some of you may not be familiar with the ministry of Jackie Pullinger. She is originally from England.[102] At the age of 20 God called her to work as a missionary in the Walled City in Hong Kong.[103] Her work in that city has continued for over 40 years. Jackie's work has focused largely on reaching

---

[102] Jackie Pullinger with Andrew Quicke, *Chasing the Dragon: One Woman's Struggle Against the Darkness of Hong Kong's Drug Dens* (Ventura, CA: Regal Books, 2006), 26, 36.
[103] Ibid., back cover.

out to hoods, prostitutes, and drug addicts.[104] Her story is told in the book, *Chasing the Dragon*, and also in the DVD, *The Law of Love*. In *Chasing the Dragon* she tells the story how she happened to settle on Hong Kong as her mission field.

When Jackie was considering the idea of missionary service, she had a dream in which her family was gathered around a map of Africa.[105] In the midst of this map there was a pink-colored country called Hong Kong.[106] She did not think that was where Hong Kong was really located, but she did not want to appear ignorant.[107] She said something about it and her Aunty Dotty, who was in the dream, assured her that that was where Hong Kong was located.[108]

The dream was not the only thing that led Jackie to Hong Kong. As she traveled trying to figure out where God wanted her to serve she was struck by the sight of the city.[109] When she saw it, she knew that this was where she was supposed to be.[110] However, I believe the dream was significant, because she did end up in Hong Kong, and she has had many years of productive ministry there. We know that Hong Kong is not located in Africa, but seeing it there on the map in her dream helped to highlight it to her. Before she had the dream, Jackie said that when she thought about doing missions work she wrote to various agencies in Africa because, in her words, "that's where missionaries go."[111] Looking at a map of Africa, where she thought missionaries went, and finding Hong Kong there was an early sign to her that she should go there.

Summary

In this chapter we have seen two of the significant ways in which the Lord uses dreams today. The first concerned salvation. The Lord has drawn

---

[104] Ibid.
[105] Ibid., 32.
[106] Ibid.
[107] Ibid.
[108] Ibid.
[109] Ibid., 24.
[110] Ibid.
[111] Ibid., 31.

people to himself through dreams. We did not find specific examples of this when we studied the dreams in the New Testament. However, we did see it with reference to visions. Saul of Tarsus became a believer in Jesus through a vision (Acts 26:12-19). Also, Cornelius' vision of an angel ultimately led to his salvation and that of his relatives and friends (Acts 10:3; 24, 44-46; 11:14-17). Though we cannot point to a New Testament text in which the Lord used a dream to draw someone to himself, it is clear from some of the accounts in this chapter that the Lord is using dreams to draw people to salvation. I mentioned in the introduction of this book that many people in Muslim lands are converted through dreams. These are places where Christianity is not the dominant religion. In fact, in some of these places, a person can be persecuted or killed for being a Christian. Would these people have come to faith in Jesus without these dreams? We cannot say for sure. It may be that they needed to have a powerful supernatural experience in order to bring them to faith in Jesus. The Lord knows how to reach people, and he granted these individuals dreams. The dreams resulted in the salvation of their souls; in this we rejoice.

The second use of dreams that we observed in this chapter concerned ministry. The Lord used these revelations of the night to supply his servants with information and direction. How might things have turned out differently if some of these people had not received dreams? Or what would have happened if they had not taken them seriously? Would R. Loren Sandford have gone to Denver? Would Jackie Pullinger have gone to Hong Kong? Once again, we cannot say for sure, but we can see that dreams were important in leading them to their respective fields of service. The Lord is interested in orchestrating the proper placement of his servants in his global plan.

Please note that the recipients of the dreams in this chapter included both men and women. Also please note that those who received the dreams came from both Eastern and Western hemispheres. Philip Jenkins has written that dreams are a basic part of the Christian faith in the global South.[112] The fact that some of the accounts in this chapter come from the

---

[112] Jenkins, 7-8.

West (and North) should encourage Western Christians that God-given dreams are for us too. Dreams are not geographically limited; they are a global phenomenon for the people of God. It is not our location in the world that limits dreams; it is, at least in part, our lack of expectation and faith that dreams are a real way in which the Lord communicates with his people.

Visions

In the last chapter I said that it was not my intention to provide an extensive list of God-given dreams throughout the history of the Christian faith. The same holds true in this chapter about visions. If you are interested in accounts of the continuing nature of visions in the Christian faith, you might take a look at *Visions of Jesus* by Chet and Lucile Huyssen. The authors have collected accounts of visions from a number of different sources so that they are accessible in one volume. This is an older book that may be difficult to find (though at the time of this writing there were still some copies available online).

In the process of studying the biblical passages for this book, I learned an important truth. Prior to my study, I was not entirely convinced that a mental picture qualified as a vision. I thought of a vision as an experience that eclipsed one's present reality; that is, when the Lord gave a person a vision, it filled the person's line of sight, and the realities of the present world were temporarily blocked out. This is most certainly a vision, one which Randy Clark would call an open vision.[113] However, after studying Paul's vision of Ananias in Acts 9:12, I have come to the conclusion that a mental picture can rightfully be called a vision. When Paul saw Ananias, at that time Paul was physically blind. The only way he could have seen him then would have been in his mind's eye, that is, via a mental picture. The fact that Paul's experience is called a vision and that what he saw actually came to pass demonstrates that mental pictures are a way in which the Lord communicates. You will find at least one account of this kind of vision in this chapter. What was true in the first century is also true today.

---

[113] Bill Johnson and Randy Clark, *The Essential Guide to Healing: Equipping All Christians to Pray for the Sick* (Minneapolis, MN: Chosen Books, 2011), 28.

Nancy Hudson

In the last chapter we looked at a dream that played an important part in Nancy's life. Though she did not understand it at first, her friend's interpretation of it proved to be true. Below you will find the account of a vision that Nancy received. This vision led to her salvation. The account below comes from an email she sent to me on January 2, 2012.

> About a year before I was saved, around 1980, I was starting to doze off one evening on my living room couch. It was dark, and all of a sudden it lit up outside so much so that my living room was in a bright light. I knew I wasn't dreaming because I wasn't asleep. I looked out my big picture window and saw multitudes of people in white going up in the air. I saw my grandmother coming toward me walking across a green meadow in a dress she always wore. I could clearly smell her perfume. She said, "Come, Nancy," and put her arms out. All of those who were going up had their arms in the air, and I just knew if I did that I would surely die. It all scared me so badly that I bolted upright on my couch, and then the light went out. I was sitting in pitch darkness wondering what on earth had just happened.

> The next day, my born-again sister came to visit me. I told her I had a funny dream, but that I was not sleeping. She said, "Nan, you had a vision of the rapture." I had no clue what she was talking about. She left and came back with a tract about the rapture. As I read the tract, I got out an old Bible and looked up 1 Thessalonians 4:16-17; after I had I read it, I realized that this is what I had seen. Now, I had never heard of the rapture, so it wasn't anything I would have pictured as a Christian does. The natural mind does not understand things of the Spirit, so I was still scared and didn't want to

touch the subject.

During the course of the next year, I kept receiving tracts in the mail; people witnessed to me, and a lot of people praying for me. I finally consented to go to an outreach with a friend where I witnessed people singing in tongues, hands up in the air, and joy. I eventually got saved through the ministry of Pastor Geno Demarco with whom I had gone to high school. I just went on with the Lord from there. I have shared this vision many times throughout the years, and it has led many to Jesus.

Katie Pawlak

Katie Pawlak attends The River Church in Waltham, Massachusetts. In a service in early 2012, she shared the story of a vision she received a few years earlier. At the time she received the vision she attended Community of Faith Christian Fellowship in Brighton, Massachusetts. Community of Faith Christian Fellowship planted The River Church in 2010. I asked her to put her vision in writing for me; the account below comes from an email she sent to me on February 26, 2012.

In February 2008, I attended a missions conference put on by our church. During one of the conference worship sessions, I closed my eyes and saw a vivid picture of my husband Dan (who played drums for our church) sitting in a circle of African men, all of whom were playing drums together. I shared this image with Dan later that evening, and neither of us had any explanation or meaning for the vision at the time. Several months later, we had the opportunity to join a team of church members on a mission trip to Uganda, where we would be working with a team of Americans and Ugandan refugees to build orphanage homes and harvest crops. Every morning, the Ugandans and Americans met for a time of worship and Bible teaching before starting the work day. The worship was accompanied by a variety of percussion instruments, including a traditional cowhide hand drum played by two men sitting back to back on the drum. On our first morning in Uganda, we learned that one of the two men who usually played this special drum was absent and they were looking for someone to fill in. My husband volunteered, and as he sat back to back with our new Ugandan friend and started to play, my mind flashed back to the vision I'd had at the conference, which was now playing out before me.

Eugene Smith

We met Eugene in the last chapter. At that time we looked at a dream he had. The dream contained his call to preach as well as a theme which would become a major emphasis of his ministry. The emphasis was the importance of knowing both the scriptures and the power of the Holy Spirit. In this chapter we will be looking at a vision he received shortly after he became a Christian. The account below comes from an email he sent to me on February 27, 2012.

> When I was about 13 or 14 years of age, I was attending a camp meeting sponsored by the Pentecostal church I was saved at. I came from a good and loving home, but not a Christian home. I therefore had no exposure to, or experience with, anything regarding the gifts or manifestations of the Holy Spirit. However, that was about to change.
>
> I had been saved only a short time through a Sunday School outreach. Shortly after that, I began to attend the church, joined the youth group, etc. During the camp meeting, the preacher had spoken about the baptism in the Holy Spirit. Along with others, I was a candidate to receive. As we waited upon the Lord, several people laid hands on me and prayed,

but nothing transpired immediately. However, shortly after that I was granted a vision that was so vivid that I can remember it to this day in great detail, some forty plus years after the fact.

In this vision, I saw myself standing on the edge of a cliff. In front of me was a great canyon, a huge valley. The entire world was gathered in the valley before me. Every nation was present. I distinctly remember seeing different cultures, different styles of dress and skin colors, as well as hearing various languages. It seemed as if the world was busy with the hustle and bustle of everyday life, buying and selling as the day required.

The only other movement I saw was the setting of the sun that started behind me, casting my shadow across anyone in front of me across the valley. Then the sun began to set, moving towards a mountain range on the other side of the valley. The sun progressed across the sky until it began to dip behind the mountains. As the sun was setting, the vision began to grow dark. When the sun had completely set behind the mountain range, the vision went completely dark and was over.

I had not yet spoken in tongues (that came later), but this vision was played out in front of me. The wall I was looking at was like a television screen, playing out the scene before me. Of course, with no experience in spiritual things, I had no clue as to what this could possibly be, never mind what it meant!

Only later in life was I made aware of the significance of this vision. I remember sharing this vision with the president of a

Bible school some years later. He immediately opened his Bible to Joel 3:13-15 which describes what I saw: multitudes, multitudes in the valley of decision, even as the sun becomes dark. More specifically, God was, like the dreams he gave to Joseph in Genesis 37, showing me what His will for my life was, though it was beyond my comprehension. In some way, my life was to touch the nations of the earth. It would be some twenty-five years later that this became a reality in my experience, as God began to open doors of ministry on several continents, and for fourteen years, I crisscrossed the globe, traveling from nation to nation, culture to culture, as a teacher of the Word of God. It has been a varied and yet wonderful experience and privilege.

The message that Eugene received in the vision was confirmed by a prophetic word he received when he was 18 years old. An account of the prophetic word is included below.

When I was eighteen, I left home to move to another city to be part of a church that I had become acquainted with. Little did I know how providential that was. Shortly after moving to this new location, the church had a special speaker come in who would later become my spiritual father and mentor. As a man who truly stood in the office of a New Testament prophet, he asked me to stand as he delivered the word of the Lord to me. By revelation of the Spirit, he told me of travel to distant places, flying on jets to foreign countries, speaking to groups of people, and then getting on another jet to travel another great distance to do the same. This man of God accurately spoke of the Lord's design for my life. It would be another twenty-two years before this prophetic would come to pass, in all the fine detail that was prophesied.

Jackie Pullinger

We also met Jackie in the last chapter. At that time we looked at a dream she had that I believe contributed in some way to bringing her to her mission field in Hong Kong. A short time after she had that dream, she also had a vision. She received it in a "tiny, peaceful village church."[114] In the vision she saw a woman holding out her arms and saying, "What can you give us?"[115] At first Jackie began to wonder what she, as a missionary, should give, but she came to realize that what the woman really needed was Jesus' love.[116] She said that if the woman had the love of Jesus, then when she had to leave, the woman would still be full, and she, in turn, could share it with others also.[117] This clarified for Jackie what the focus of her ministry would be, though at the time she was still not sure where she was supposed to go to minister.[118]

Heidi Baker

In the book *Always Enough: God's Miraculous Provision Among the Poorest Children on Earth,* Heidi Baker says that the Lord spoke to her audibly and told her that he was calling her to be a minister and missionary and that she was to go to Africa, Asia, and England.[119] All of this has come to pass. Rolland and Heidi Baker are the founders of Iris Ministries and currently serve in Mozambique, Africa; you can learn more about their ministry by visiting their website at http://www.irismin.org/.

Heidi had the call of God on her life and served him in the places he had said she would go, but she encountered some significant challenges. At one time she became particularly overwhelmed; she was exhausted and very sick.[120] She and Rolland had been working 18 hour days, and they were

---

[114] Pullinger, 32.
[115] Ibid., 33.
[116] Ibid.
[117] Ibid.
[118] Ibid.
[119] Rolland and Heidi Baker, *Always Enough: God's Miraculous Provision Among the Poorest Children on Earth* (Grand Rapids, MI: Chosen Books, 2003), 26.
[120] Ibid., 48.

caring for over 300 children.[121] It was a vision that helped her to press on. She received the vision at the Toronto Airport Christian Fellowship.[122]

In the vision Heidi saw thousands of children coming to her; she told the Lord, "No, Lord. There are too many!"[123] The Lord told her to look into his eyes and give the children something to eat.[124] She then saw the Lord take a piece of his broken body and give it to her; it turned into bread in her hands and she distributed it to the children.[125] Then the Lord told her to look into his eyes and give the children something to drink.[126] Jesus gave her a cup that contained blood and water; she drank from it and gave that to the children as well; the cup did not run out.[127] Then the Lord spoke to her and said, "There will always be enough, because I died."[128] As a result of this vision, the Bakers not only continued the work they were doing, but also expanded it. Iris Ministries now feeds more than ten thousand children each day.[129]

Loren Cunningham

Many Christians are familiar with Youth with a Mission, also know as YWAM. This is a major missionary-sending organization. If you are not familiar with this ministry, you can learn more about it on their website, http://www.ywam.org/. Though the ministry is well-known, I do not think that many people know how it came into being. A vision played a major role in the establishment of Youth with a Mission. In his book *Is That Really You God?* Loren Cunningham provides an account of it.

He was in the Bahamas at the time doing ministry as part of a gospel quartet.[130] One night after the group sang he had a vision while he was on

---

[121] Ibid.
[122] Ibid., 49.
[123] Ibid.
[124] Ibid.
[125] Ibid.
[126] Ibid.
[127] Ibid.
[128] Ibid., 50.
[129] See http://www.irismin.org/about/history.
[130] Loren Cunningham with Janice Rogers, *Is That Really You, God?* (Seattle, WA: YWAM Publishing, 2001), 31-32.

his bed in a guest room that had been provided by a missionary.[131] Like Katie Pawlak's experience, which we looked at earlier, Loren's vision came in the form of a mental picture. He described it "a mental movie."[132] He had asked the Lord to speak to him in his mind.[133] The Lord answered his request. In his mind he saw a map of the world with waves of the sea coming up on all the shores of the continents.[134] The waves would come upon the land, recede, and then come up on the land again until they eventually covered the whole continent.[135] The waves then turned into young people who were sharing the gospel on every continent.[136] When Loren had this experience, he wondered if God was showing him what he would do in the future.[137] The vision has proved to be a prophetic sign of what the ministry Loren would found would do: send young people into the whole world to preach the gospel.

Summary

In this chapter we have looked at a number of modern-day visions. These visions, like the dreams we saw in the previous chapter, were given to both men and women. One of the revelations was given to help draw a person to salvation (something God wants for everyone, 1 Tim. 2:3-4). The Lord saved Nancy Hudson, and she would later serve him. But the majority of the visions we looked at were given to people who were already Christians at the time, and the revelations they received dealt with ministry and missions. This is no surprise because that is where God's heart is. The Lord frequently reaches out to the world through his people. God is very interested in having his people serve him and accomplish his purposes. He will go to great lengths to lead and encourage them to do this. He did this in the days of the

---

[131] Ibid., 32.
[132] Ibid.
[133] Ibid.
[134] Ibid.
[135] Ibid.
[136] Ibid., 32-33.
[137] Ibid., 33.

New Testament, and he continues to do this today. If people and circumstances do not encourage you in ministry, he will.

The Lord's guidance through visions also highlights the truths that the Lord has specific works for each of his people to do and places for them to go. The supernatural guidance the Lord supplies through visions is not just for the benefit of those who minister for him, it is also for the benefit of those who will receive their ministry. Visions are one powerful way in which the Lord can direct his people.

Closing Words

In parts one and two of this book, we studied the dreams and visions of the New Testament. It was interesting to see how the Lord so marvelously intervened in the lives of the biblical characters. As a result of our study, we also gained some understanding of how the Lord worked through dreams and visions. The same God who gave these revelations back then still exists today. It is, therefore, not unreasonable to expect that he will continue to use dreams and visions in our day as means of communicating with humanity.

Part three of the book confirmed that God does indeed still speak through these means. We looked at some modern-day accounts of dreams and visions. These were real revelations, given to different people at different times. Each proved to be relevant and helpful to those who received them.

I dedicated this book to "rekindling expectations for divinely inspired dreams and visions among people in the West." Some of the testimonies in chapters 20 and 21 demonstrate that these things do take place in the West. Dreams and visions do not belong exclusively to the Eastern hemisphere or the global South. God is not bound by geography! His activities are global. Ultimately, God decides who receives dreams and visions. Nevertheless, I think that we would find them more prevalent in the West if we were more open to them.

So what can we do in order to reclaim the experience of divinely-inspired dreams and visions? Below are a few suggestions that may help move us in the right direction. We need to realize that

1. God gave dreams and visions in biblical times.
2. The Lord has not changed (Mal. 3:6; Heb. 13:8).
3. The things he did in the past he can still do today.
4. We live in a time in which these things are to be expected (Acts 2:17).

5. We are still in need of divine guidance.

6. The anti-supernaturalistic views that surround us do not come from the Bible.

If we remind ourselves of these truths and seek to live in simple faith toward

the Lord, I would not be surprised to find that he has rekindled the experience of divinely inspired dreams and visions in the West. O, Lord, make it so!

I hope that wherever you live your faith has been stirred to a greater expectation that the Lord can communicate with you in one of these ways. After all, these are biblical experiences, and now is the time!

> In the last days, God says, I will pour out my Spirit on all people. Your sons and daughters will prophesy, your young men will see visions, your old men will dream dreams. (Acts 2:17)

Bibliography

Baker, Rolland, and Heidi Baker. *Always Enough: God's Miraculous Provision Among the Poorest Children on Earth.* Grand Rapids, MI: Chosen Books, 2003.

Bock, Darrell L. *Luke 1:1–9:50.* Baker Exegetical Commentary on the New Testament. Grand Rapids, MI: Baker Books, 1994.

Cunningham, Loren, with Janice Rogers. *Is That Really You, God?* Seattle, WA: YWAM Publishing, 2001.

Deere, Jack. *Surprised by the Power of the Spirit.* Grand Rapids, MI: Zondervan Publishing House, 1993.

Fee, Gordon D. *Gospel and Spirit: Issues in New Testament Hermeneutics.* Peabody, MA: Hendrickson Publishers, 1991.

Fee, Gordon D., and Douglas Stuart. *How to Read the Bible for All It's Worth.* Grand Rapids, MI: Zondervan Publishing House, 1993.

Green, Joel B., Scott McKnight, and I. Howard Marshall, eds. *Dictionary of Jesus and the Gospels.* Downers Grove, IL: InterVarsity Press, 1992.

Greeson, Kevin. *The Camel: How Muslims Are Coming to Faith in Christ.* Arkadelphia, AR: WIGtake Resources, LLC, 2007.

Heidler, Robert. *Experiencing the Spirit.* Ventura, CA: Regal Books, 1998.

Hyun, KeumJu Jewel, and Cynthia Davis Lathrop. *Some Men Are Our Heroes: Stories by Women About the Men Who Have Greatly Influenced Their Lives.* Euguene, OR: Wipf and Stock Publishers, 2010.

Jenkins, Philip. *The Next Christendom: The Coming of Global Christianity.* New York, NY: Oxford University Press, 2002.

Jersak, Brad. *Can You Hear Me?: Tuning in to the God Who Speaks.* Oxford, UK, Grand Rapids, MI: Monarch Press, 2006.

Johnson, Bill, and Randy Clark. *The Essential Guide to Healing: Equipping All Christians to Pray for the Sick.* Minneapolis, MN: Chosen Books, 2011.

Keener, Craig S. *A Commentary on the Gospel of Matthew.* Grand Rapids, MI: Wm. B. Eerdmans Publishing Company, 1999.

_____. *Gift & Giver: The Holy Spirit for Today.* Grand Rapids, MI: Baker Academic, 2001.

_____. *1–2 Corinthians.* The New Cambridge Bible Commentary. New York: NY: Cambridge University Press, 2005.

_____. *The IVP Bible Background Commentary: New Testament.* Downers Grove, IL: InterVarsity Press, 1993.

Kelsey, Morton. *Dreams: A Way to Listen to God.* New York: NY: Paulist Press, 1978.

Lathrop, John P. *Apostles, Prophets, Evangelists, Pastors, and Teachers Then and Now.* Maitland, FL: Xulon Press, 2008.

McReynolds, Paul R. *Word Study Greek-English New Testament.* Wheaton, IL: Tyndale House Publishers, 1998.

Pullinger, Jackie, with Andrew Quicke. *Chasing the Dragon: One Woman's Struggle Against the Darkness of Hong Kong's Drug Dens.* Ventura, CA: Regal Books, 2006.

Ryken, Leland, and James C. Wilhoit, et al., eds. *The Dictionary of Biblical Imagery.* Downers Grove, IL: InterVarsity Press, 1998.

Stott, John. *The Spirit, the Church, and the World.* Downers Grove, IL: InterVarsity Press, 1990.

Sullivant, Michael. *Prophetic Etiquette.* Lake Mary, FL: Charisma House, 2000.

Walvoord, John F., and Roy B. Zuck, eds. *The Bible Knowledge Commentary: New Testament.* Wheaton, IL: Victor Books, 1983.

Witherington, Ben III. *The Acts of the Apostles: A Socio-Rhetorical Commentary.* Grand Rapids, MI: Wm. B. Eerdmans Publishing Company, 1998.

Yaraei, Kamran. *Testimony.* DVD. Fort Mill, SC: Morningstar Ministries, 2005.

www.ingramcontent.com/pod-product-compliance
Lightning Source LLC
Chambersburg PA
CBHW051832040426
42447CB00006B/492